"Across public services, our ability to gener[...] gies that work, consistently and sustainabl[...] innovations. Algorithms, artificial intellig[...] are starting to reshape the world around us but technological innovations in how best to spend billions of pounds of public money receives only a fraction of the attention. Some will point to political processes, project management or 'evidence-based policy making' as the way this should be done, but all of them fail to address the fundamental question: who is really in charge? *From Woe to Flow* and OpenStrategies answers this question head on: we, the public, are in charge because if we can't or don't want to use what is provided, for whatever reason, then we will not. Keeping the focus firmly on 'Uses', the OpenStrategies PRUB system offers an advanced approach to systematically building insight, wisdom and local knowledge of citizens and service users into strategies. It helps decision makers avoid expensive white elephants steering them instead towards properly informed decisions about where to put effort and money. It is a tool for the modern era – one in which people are respected and institutions coproduce services with citizens. It could also save you a lot of time and heartache."

– Merron Simpson, CEO, New NHS Alliance

"Public institutions usually operate in a complex context that involve many stakeholders. We have all seen several programs and organisations working towards very similar goals, seemingly with little coordination between them. OpenStrategies breaks strategy down to its essence and offers a common language for doing so: your organisation does projects, that lead to results and (only!) when these results are put to use you achieve the intended benefits. The world may is complex enough, so we really need a simple method so we can work towards a mutual understanding of what we are working towards. And more importantly: what we are actually doing to achieve our goals."

– Edo Plantinga, independent program manager for the
Dutch digital government

"This is a book that delivers valuable insight into the 'what', 'how' and 'why' of an actionable strategy system within a complex environment. The author helpfully develops a 9-stage process, which equips you with a common language to successfully implement

OpenStrategies which ultimately create sustainable benefits. It also addresses the importance of accountability in a meaningful and democratic way, shifting the emphasis from 'who' you are accountable to, to 'what' you are accountable for. I have no hesitation in recommending this book to practitioners, students and academics seeking an alternative and more nuanced understanding of strategy to the orthodoxy."

– Dr Rebecca Casey, Newcastle University, UK

From Woe to Flow

Large-scale, complex systems like the health sector or transport are a challenge to manage; traditional strategic approaches often fail due to the diversity of different stakeholders and the lack of a cohesive strategy language that all within it can understand. What is needed in such systems is a new, fresh, scalable, 'open source' framework: one that is 'editable' by those at all levels within the organisation.

This book provides practitioners and managers within any organisation with a 9-stage modular toolkit for all strategic steps. Utilising Phil Driver's PRUB framework, which innovatively centres on end-user actions instead of benefits – what do you want to do? – it enables all stakeholders from entry level to executive to actively participate in strategy validation and implementation. This book will enable practitioners with skills in any one of the 9 stages to enhance their skills in that stage but also, most importantly, to link their work in any one stage with all the other stages. The book will also help senior executives to coordinate the full 9-stage sequence in large-scale and complex environments.

Following on from Phil Driver's groundbreaking *Validating Strategies*, this book covers all 9 stages of strategy, from end-user engagement through to post-implementation review. It will prove game-changing reading for any manager, executive or practitioner that needs a more effective strategic approach, manages a large or complex system in the public sector, or wants to enable and empower talent at all levels of their organisation.

Phil Driver is founder and CEO of OpenStrategies Ltd. His background in science and engineering management led to his involvement in large-scale industry-sector strategies. That in turn led to his developing an in-depth understanding of the challenges of even larger scale, public sector strategies. The OpenStrategies' system then evolved through more than a decade of intense engagement with many public and private sector organisations.

From Woe to Flow

Validating and Implementing Strategies

PHIL DRIVER

Routledge
Taylor & Francis Group

LONDON AND NEW YORK

First published 2020 by Routledge

2 Park Square, Milton Park, Abingdon, Oxon OX14 4RN

605 Third Avenue, New York, NY 10017

Routledge is an imprint of the Taylor & Francis Group, an informa business

First issued in paperback 2022

Publisher's Note

The publisher has gone to great lengths to ensure the quality of this reprint but points out that some imperfections in the original copies may be apparent.

British Library Cataloguing-in-Publication Data
A catalogue record for this book is available from the British Library

Library of Congress Cataloging-in-Publication Data
A catalog record has been requested for this book

ISBN: 978-1-138-59862-1 (hbk)
ISBN: 978-1-03-233720-3 (pbk)
DOI: 10.4324/9780429486258

Typeset in Palatino Linotype
by Deanta Global Publishing Services, Chennai, India

Contents

List of Figures

List of Tables

Foreword for *From Woe to Flow*

In the early part of the 19th century, the Rosetta Stone enabled Jean-François Champollion to decipher the Egyptian hieroglyphs and in doing so he opened our eyes to the rich culture of an ancient world.

Phil Driver's writing, both his 2014 title, *Validating Strategies*, and now this new volume, *From Woe to Flow*, are, at least in business and management terms, equally transformational; creating a language and a grammar that enables us to understand and manage the world of complex projects.

The accelerating number and scale of major projects and the aspirations of the strategies behind them have left traditional project management struggling to keep up. Whereas in the 20th century projects were the vehicle for producing tangible outputs in the form of *products* or *buildings*, or *easily definable objectives* (to reach the moon or eliminate leprosy), the emphasis of major projects in the 21st century has turned to *Benefits*; the value that citizens and indeed society draw from our investments in time and money . The expression of this value requires a language and indeed a culture to give it form.

It is for this new language and the culture with which it is associated that Phil Driver's PRUB-Logic provides us all with a primer.

Validating Strategies established the logic and the process for articulating strategies and delivering them coherently as projects. The focus of Phil's new book *From Woe to Flow* is the supply chain in a typical project. With the same engineering precision that he brought to his earlier work, he analyses the role of the client, the supplier and the end user in building efficiency (in terms of project management and use-design) and effectiveness (in terms of project outputs and the benefits and value associated with their adoption). In doing so, he clarifies the roles and explains where and how accountabilities lie.

The result is a rich and convincing guide that informs many of the key aspects of complex project management: the requirements of users; the knowledge and insight that lies within the supply chain; the value thread that is woven throughout the project's lifecycle and how this can be effectively represented and supported through contracts based on outputs and supplier performance; ultimately the basis for measuring and improving the performance of strategies and the projects that underpin them.

In simple terms *Validating Strategies* and *From Woe to Flow* enable organisations:

- to prioritise their investments by understanding whether a strategy is deliverable and whether it is worth the effort
- to recast the relationship between client, supplier and user – which is a theme that underpins a huge amount of current academic and practitioner activity including The Institution of Civil Engineer's Project 13, the Constructing Excellence Network and much of the work of the UK's National Infrastructure Commission
- to reframe projects from a limited and linear set of activities to a virtuous circular activity that extends along the complete lifecycle of design, delivery, operation, reuse or decommissioning and then, through the benefits associated with performance measurement and improvement, back to design

Phil Driver's arguments are often detailed but they never become over-complicated. By focusing on the fundamental relationship between projects, their outputs (or results), the behaviour of the users and the value of what they generate, he effectively captures the *essence of project management*: to what we aspire, in terms of what we can do or be as an organisation or a society. Which neatly leaves *the how*; the choice of what to create and how to facilitate it, firmly where it belongs, with the businesses and governments who make the strategic decisions on project initiation.

Jonathan Norman, Manager, Major Projects
Knowledge Hub, Major Projects Association

Implementing Validated Strategies – from Woe to Flow

Preface and Acknowledgements

This book is a practitioner's guide to the strategy development and implementation processes that were defined in *Validating Strategies, Linking Projects and Results to Uses and Benefits* (https://www.routledge.com/products/9781472427816).

The book's purpose is to guide the seamless transition from ideas through to strategies, investment decisions, contracting, implementation, performance management and strategy review. The book is based on the succinct strategy logic called PRUB-Logic.

PRUB-Logic represents the universal sequence:

> **P**rojects create **R**esults that enable and motivate **U**ses to create **B**enefits.

PRUB-Logic Uses: "the smallest amount of strategic information that has the highest value to the most stakeholders".

When stakeholders all use this straightforward strategy logic in each stage of the above sequence it enables effective communications between groups of stakeholders and helps eliminate groups 'working in silos'.

Strategies based on PRUB-Logic and the overall OpenStrategies system can be implemented with confidence because they have been *Validated* and are readily understood by everyone involved.

This book describes and demonstrates the practical Uses of PRUB-Logic in a 9-stage sequence from initial engagement with end users/customers through to strategy implementation and review.

This book does not describe specific methodologies for actions such as stakeholder engagement or project management as these are already well documented elsewhere. Instead, this book focuses on the *information-content* (the PRUB-Logic) of these actions and how this strategy logic enables stakeholders to create strategies that really will 'enable and motivate Uses to create Benefits'.

Thank you to all the multi-stakeholder groups who have shared their diverse and complex challenges with our network of Validating Strategies Practitioners. Through these groups, we have learnt an enormous amount about what does and does not work in large and complex strategic environments. We have then been generously permitted by our clients to test our OpenStrategies approach to create, *Validate* and implement effective strategies. We continue to refine OpenStrategies through our ongoing work with these groups.

I really appreciate the detailed editorial feedback that my daughter Rosie Oliver gave me on an early draft of this book. Other colleagues who have provided helpful feedback include Clare Sherwood, Ian Seath, Dan Randow, Helen Telford, Merron Simpson and Merv Wyeth. However, I take full responsibility for the final version of this book.

Merron Simpson, Merv Wyeth and Helen Telford are Validating Strategies Practitioners who have provided me with a regular flow of high-quality feedback from their stakeholder groups and this has helped underpin many of the practical tips in this book.

Professor Simone Fuhles-Ubach at the Cologne University of Science Technology and the Arts in Germany, Professor Piet Beukman at Canterbury University in New Zealand and Rebecca Casey at Newcastle University in the UK have given me many opportunities to teach OpenStrategies to hundreds of their Masters-level students. These students have assertively expressed their opinions about OpenStrategies and these perspectives have led to further refinements to OpenStrategies and the manner in which we teach it. We have had a lot of fun doing this, especially coming up with stimulating workshop exercises.

I particularly appreciate the ongoing patience and practical and moral support from my wife Christine Moore during the long gestation of this book.

Different readers of this book will feel 'at home' in different stages in the OpenStrategies system. For example, specialists in stakeholder engagement will probably feel most at home in Stages 1–2 (Chapters 4–5); strategists will be most comfortable in Stages 2–4 (Chapters 5–7); and project managers will probably feel most at home in Stages 6–8 (Chapters 9–11). Such specialists may wish to read this book by starting with introductory chapters 1–3 and then read the chapter that is most relevant to their *current* roles. However, I encourage readers to then read the chapters either side of their current areas of expertise so as to see how their current work fits into the full sequence from initial stakeholder engagement through strategies, contracts, implementation and review. Finally, readers may wish to distil the 9 × 1-page summaries of each stage in the OpenStrategies system as condensed in chapter 13.

Chapter 1

Introduction

This book describes the OpenStrategies system for seamlessly developing and refining *strategic information* from the initial collection of strategic ideas from end-users, through 9 stages including strategy development, implementation, performance management and strategy review. The detailed mechanisms for running each stage (e.g. focus groups; Agile; project management etc.) are outside the realm of this book which focuses on the *strategic information content* of each stage.

Throughout the 9 OpenStrategies stages described in this book, the focus is on what each stage needs to achieve in order to enable all the other 8 stages and in particular the subsequent stage.

The OpenStrategies system is based on PRUB-Logic, where PRUB represents the universal sequence:

> **P**rojects create **R**esults that enable and motivate **U**ses to create **B**enefits. This PRUB-Logic aligns with the sequence: create assets (outputs) and enable their Uses to create Benefits (outcomes).

The OpenStrategies system addresses the need for a start-to-finish strategy system that enables and motivates all stakeholders to develop and implement strategies in large and complex environments. The OpenStrategies system:

1. Uses a simple strategy language that all stakeholders can understand.
2. Demonstrates how inputs (Projects) link through Results and Uses to Benefits and that there are no shortcuts from Projects to Benefits.

3.   Clearly defines accountabilities for each and every stakeholder.

4.   Enables the seamless transition from ideas generation through 9 stages of strategy development and implementation to final review and updating of strategies.

So, what is the problem that OpenStrategies addresses?

In our conversations with thousands of individuals in the public, private and third sectors we hear their views that less than 20% of strategies have any impact.

Why is this?

As described in detail in my previous book *Validating Strategies* we have concluded that:

- Life is not as simple as 'create a strategy then implement it'.
- The real world is *complex* (full of unknown-unknowns as defined by Snowden and Boone – Harvard Business Review Reprint R0711C) and full of uncertainties
- However, strategies and actions must necessarily be *simple* (known-knowns). You can only implement what you know you are going to implement even if there is uncertainty about subsequent effects and impacts
- It can be challenging to translate between the complexity of the real world and the simplicity necessary for effective actions.
- Complexity includes multiple stakeholders; multiple agendas; multiple and diverse end-users, suppliers, purchasers and strategic ideas; the need for many different people with diverse skills to simultaneously understand and implement different levels of strategies.
- We need a full-spectrum strategy system that simultaneously addresses *all* of the above issues
- We have identified 9 distinct stages that stakeholders need to work through from an initial idea to the successful completion and review of a strategy:
  1.   Stage 1 – Understand Uses and Benefits: engage with end-users to determine what they want to do and why
  2.   Stage 2 – Understand Projects and Results: engage with service suppliers to determine what they can potentially provide

3. Stage 3 – Develop Evidence-based strategies: create logical, Evidence-based SubStrategies aligning user requirements with suppliers' insights

4. Stage 4 – Validate SubStrategies by determining their Worth: determine both their Global Worth and their Motivational Worth (as defined in Chapter 7).

5. Stage 5 – Make investment decisions: compare SubStrategies and select the best ones for investment.

6. Stage 6 – Develop performance-based contracts: incorporate Validated SubStrategies and performance indicators and targets into robust contracts.

7. Stage 7 – Implement strategies: follow the PRUB-Logic sequence to implement strategies

8. Stage 8 – Performance-manage strategies: use measurements of indicators to guide the *Efficient* implementation of *current* strategies.

9. Stage 9 – Review and update strategies: review the *Effectiveness* of current strategies and update them where appropriate.

- Each and every stage needs to be clearly elucidated so everyone can understand it
- Strategic information needs to flow seamlessly between each and every one of these *stages*.
- Different stakeholders are involved in each of the 9 stages so the strategic information needs to flow seamlessly between many *stakeholders*
- Stakeholders need to produce chunks of information in each stage that suits the audience in the subsequent stage. This means that each stage needs to be especially understandable by the stakeholders in the previous stage, in the stage itself and in the subsequent stage.
- There are constraints on the viable size of the chunks of strategic information. Strategies and business systems must work with the fact that humans have cognitive limits:
    - Miller's law states that humans can hold just 7 +/– 2 ideas in their heads at any one time (https://en.wikipedia.org/wiki/The_Magical_Number_Seven,_Plus_or_Minus_Two);

- Driver's law states that humans can cope with just 15+/–5 concepts in diagrammatic form (see *Validating Strategies*).
- So, strategies need to be 'chunked' into bite-sized units of 15+/–5 concepts so the information can be readily shared and understood
- There may be multiple such chunks of information, and multiple layers of chunks of information, but each chunk must contain no more than 15 +/– 5 pieces of information.
- Stakeholders often have minimal 'strategy' knowledge (although many stakeholders think they know what strategy is and that anyone can create a strategy) so they need an ultra-simple 'strategy language' which produces:

the smallest amount of strategic information

that has the highest value

to the most stakeholders

- This requires a common strategy language that everyone understands and which works in every one of the 9 stages.
- This in turn means that stakeholders involved in any or all 9 of the above stages must *all speak the same strategy language* so they can most effectively communicate and interlink their respective activities.
- Ideally this means that *the same or similar information can be used and reused for 9 separate but seamlessly interlinked purposes.*
- There are important distinctions between:
    - identifying an issue;
    - prioritising an issue;
    - contractually specifying what will be done about an issue;
    - actually doing what is required including performance management of the issue.
- Someone needs to be accountable for all these aspects of strategy development and implementation and that accountability needs to be clear and closely linked to the strategies themselves.
- As was demonstrated in *Validating Strategies*, only Uses create Benefits – project managers cannot 'realise Benefits' – so strategies need to *enable and motivate Uses to create those Benefits.*

- Note the crucial distinction between 'users' and 'Uses'. It is Uses, by users, that create Benefits. Just because there are users does not mean they will undertake the Uses. Hence the emphasis throughout OpenStrategies on understanding what Uses will actually happen rather than simply identifying users and what they 'want'.
- Strategies need to be 'Worth it' if they are to be implemented. They need to be:
    - Globally Worth It: the value of all the Benefits must be greater than all the costs that will be incurred to enable the Benefits (see the glossary in this book);
    - Motivationally Worth It: each stakeholder who needs to contribute to the strategy needs to receive sufficient Benefits to motivate them to make that contribution.
- The world keeps changing so most strategies need to be constantly updated. Hence any strategy system must be flexible enough to be quickly reviewed and updated and for all stakeholders to know about and understand the updates.

With all the above challenges, is it any wonder that so few strategies successfully make it through all the 9 stages to achieve the desired Benefits? What is needed is a 'Full-Spectrum Strategy System' which simultaneously addresses *all* these challenges.

This book defines such a full-spectrum strategy system, that is, the OpenStrategies system based on PRUB-Logic:

Projects create Results that people Use to create Benefits

This rigorous PRUB-Logic structure providing a robust basis for addressing each and every element of the 9 stages defined above while seamlessly interlinking them into a complete, 'full-spectrum OpenStrategies system'. This means that stakeholder engagement, strategy development, business cases, investment decisions, contracts, strategy implementation, performance management and strategy review and updating are coherently connected rather than being siloed sets of actions which are untethered to any coherent thinking structure.

PRUB exactly represents reality because it represents the universal role of organisations and their customers/clients/citizens which is to:

Create assets (outputs) that people use to create outcomes
i.e.*Projects create Results that people Use to create Benefits*

Create = **P**rojects
Assets/outputs = **R**esults
Use = **U**ses
Outcomes = **B**enefits

PRUB-Logic confirms that there are no shortcuts from inputs (Projects) to outcomes (Benefits). To be successful, implementation of a strategy/contract *must* follow the sequence: *Projects create Results that people Use to create Benefits.*

We developed the full-spectrum OpenStrategies system for the most complex situation of multiple stakeholders with multiple agendas, multiple and diverse end-users, suppliers, purchasers and strategic ideas. However, it can be equally well applied to single stakeholders developing and implementing strategies on single ideas as simple as an individual strategically buying a new fishing rod or car.

A key factor is that the concept of *enabling and motivating Uses to create Benefits* should pervade all 9 stages of the OpenStrategies system.

For clarity in the following chapters, I have distilled factors associated with each individual stage while acknowledging that they are all inherently interconnected. It is worth noting that while the 9 stages have been presented here as a start-to-finish sequence, in many situations there will already be strategies being implemented but perhaps not as effectively and efficiently as desired. Therefore, it is possible for stakeholders to start anywhere in the 9-stage process and to work backwards and forwards in order to address all the actions in each of the 9 stages.

Although the fact there are 9 stages may seem a bit daunting, the reality is that every stage is based on the same simple PRUB-Logic. This means that you do not need to learn a new set of jargon or approaches to logical thinking for each stage – you just need to reuse PRUB-Logic in new ways in each stage.

Chapter 2 re-introduces PRUB-Logic which is explained in more detail in *Validating Strategies – Linking Projects and Results to Uses and Benefits.*

Chapter 3 applies PRUB-Logic to accountability to create a system of 'full-spectrum accountability'. This chapter defines a matrix of accountabilities covering effectiveness and efficiency accountabilities on one dimension and on the other dimension the four stages of accountably: identifying, prioritising, contractually specifying and performance-managing issues. It also emphasises that being 'accountable for' is far more important than being 'accountable to'. This chapter usefully distinguishes between lead indicators of Projects and Results (measures of *progress*) and lag indicators of Uses and Benefits (measures of *success*).

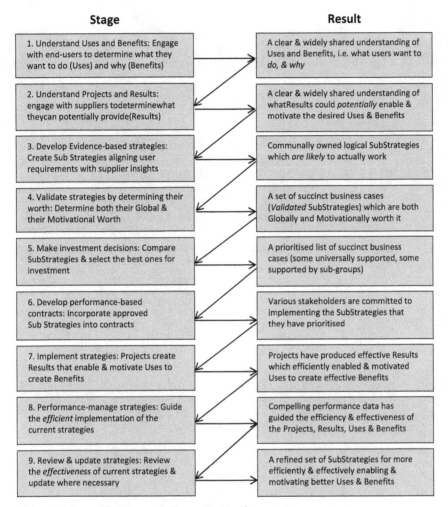

Stage   **Result**

Stage	Result
1. Understand Uses and Benefits: Engage with end-users to determine what they want to do (Uses) and why (Benefits)	A clear & widely shared understanding of Uses and Benefits, i.e. what users want to *do, & why*
2. Understand Projects and Results: engage with suppliers todeterminewhat theycan potentially provide(Results)	A clear & widely shared understanding of whatResults could *potentially* enable & motivate the desired Uses & Benefits
3. Develop Evidence-based strategies: Create Sub Strategies aligning user requirements with supplier insights	Communally owned logical SubStrategies which *are likely* to actually work
4. Validate strategies by determining their worth: Determine both their Global & their Motivational Worth	A set of succinct business cases (*Validated* SubStrategies) which are both Globally and Motivationally worth it
5. Make investment decisions: Compare SubStrategies & select the best ones for investment	A prioritised list of succinct business cases (some universally supported, some supported by sub-groups)
6. Develop performance-based contracts: Incorporate approved Sub Strategies into contracts	Various stakeholders are committed to implementing the SubStrategies that they have prioritised
7. Implement strategies: Projects create Results that enable & motivate Uses to create Benefits	Projects have produced effective Results which efficiently enabled & motivated Uses to create effective Benefits
8. Performance-manage strategies: Guide the *efficient* implementation of the current strategies	Compelling performance data has guided the efficiency & effectiveness of the Projects, Results, Uses & Benefits
9. Review & update strategies: Review the *effectiveness* of current strategies & update where necessary	A refined set of SubStrategies for more efficiently & effectively enabling & motivating better Uses & Benefits

Figure 1.1   The 9 stage OpenStrategies system.

Chapters 4 to 12 address each of the 9 stages in turn by defining them, explaining their importance, clarifying the steps necessary in each stage, demonstrating these steps with some evolving worked examples of SubStrategies based on PRUB-Logic and identifying the accountabilities associated with each stage.

Chapter 13 summarises this book and provides a succinct checklist for each of the 9 stages as shown in Figure 1.1 below.

Finally, a glossary defines the terms used in the OpenStrategies PRUB-Logic system.

Chapter 2

A brief primer on the OpenStrategies system

This chapter summarises my earlier book: *Validating Strategies – Linking Projects and Results to Uses and Benefits* (https://www.routledge.com/products/9781472427816). This earlier book will be referred to as *Validating Strategies* throughout this current book.

It is challenging to effectively and efficiently manage large-scale, multi-stakeholder environments such as in the public and local government sectors and large businesses and non-government organisations. Typically, such complex environments involve many issues and stakeholders with different skill levels and interests.

In these environments, the right things happen more quickly and effectively if all strategic processes use the same language so everyone understands what is to be done and why and joins-up all their actions across agencies; across different topics; at different levels of strategy; across different end-user groups and so on.

The *Validating Strategies* system for doing this is based on our observation that, without exception, strategies guide stakeholders to:

Create assets that enable and motivate Uses to create Benefits

This statement is universally true. It describes what happens in the real world. It is true in all sectors of the economy including the private sector, the public sector and the voluntary and charity sectors.

We represent this universal sequence as

Projects create Results that enable and motivate Uses to create Benefits

This sequence is 'PRUB-Logic'. We have yet to find any situation that cannot be effectively described succinctly using PRUB-Logic (conditions apply in complex situations).

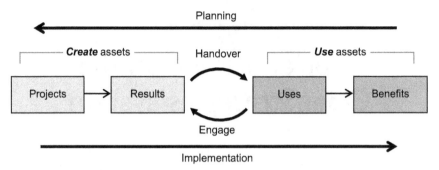

Figure 2.1   PRUB-Logic for planning and implementation.

We use upper case first letters for **P**rojects, **R**esults, **U**ses and **B**enefits (and for **S**ubStrategies, **E**vidence, **W**orths, **V**alues and **F**undamental **P**rinciples) because they have specific meanings in the OpenStrategies' system (see the Glossary in *Validating Strategies* and at the end of this book).

As shown previously in Figure 1.1, strategic thinking or planning starts with identifying Uses, then the Benefits that arise from the Uses and then identifying the set of necessary and sufficient Results that will both enable and motivate the Uses to create the Benefits. Finally, PRUB-Logic identifies the Projects necessary to create the Results. So, planning follows the sequence UBRP, or possibly BURP. This sequence keeps the Uses and users (citizens; clients; customers; the environment) at the centre of strategic planning and implementation.

Subsequently, business plans, investment decision making, contracts, implementation and performance management simply follow the PRUB-Logic sequence from Projects to Results to Uses to Benefits.

PRUB-Logic focuses primarily on *actions* (Projects and Uses) and the consequences of those actions (Results and Benefits).

The secondary focus of PRUB-Logic is on *who* does the actions. PRUB-Logic applies irrespective of who the actors are. For example, people who use a community hall for a dance festival (end-users undertaking Uses) may be the same people who paint the hall (end-users running a Project).

> *Strategies whose information structures are based primarily on actions and consequence (what needs to be done and why) remain coherent irrespective of what individual stakeholders do (who does what). In contrast: Strategies whose information structure is based primarily on stakeholders and their missions (who does what) rapidly become convoluted and fragmented and lose focus on actions and consequences (what needs to be done and why).*

A PRUB-Logic sequence generally consists of one or more Projects generating one or more Results enabling and motivating one or more Uses to create one or more Benefits.

Such a PRUB-Logic sequence is a 'SubStrategy'.

SubStrategies

Figure 2.2 shows an example of a simple SubStrategy.

This hypothetical SubStrategy shows the unbroken links from Projects (inputs) via Results (outputs) and Uses to Benefits (outcomes) while noting that the first two Results (Orphan Results – see below) feed back into Projects.

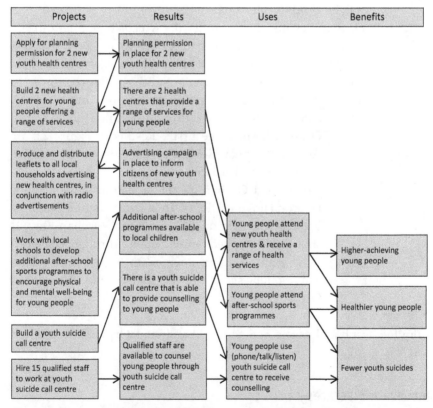

Figure 2.2   An example SubStrategy on youth health, based on prior market research that identified exactly what youth centres were required to do.

An overall strategy will generally contain a suite of interlinked SubStrategies. For example, a 'transport strategy' may contain SubStrategies on road transport; rail transport; water-based transport and air travel. The 'road transport SubStrategy' may be structured so as to contain *sub*-SubStrategies on cycling, walking, car travel, motorcycling, heavy vehicles, public transport such as buses and so on.

Orphan Results

PRUB-Logic differentiates between:

1.   Useful Results: these are Results which can be directly used by end-users. Projects can generally *ensure* that Results will be created but they can only *influence* whether or not the Results will be Used to generate Benefits.

2.   Orphan Results: these are Results which do not get directly used by end-users but which may nevertheless be worth having provided they are 'Adopted' by other Projects which then create useful Results (see Results 1 and 2 in Figure 2.2):

   a.   A Result that end-users do not use but which is Adopted by another Project is called an 'Adopted Orphan Result'. The first 2 Results in Figure 2.2 are Adopted Orphan Results because they are 'Adopted' by the 2nd and 3rd Projects.

   b.   Abandoned Orphan Results are Results that no-one Uses and no-one Adopts. They are a waste of resources. Projects that produce Abandoned Orphan Results should be stopped immediately. Through conversations with our clients, we estimate that the percentage of public sector Projects that produce Abandoned Orphan Results ranges from 15 to 40%.

Adopted Orphan Results are good. Abandoned Orphan Results are bad.

Integrating strategy processes

All 9 stages in the sequence from stakeholder engagement through business case development, investment decision making, contracting, strategy implementation and review can be effectively based on this PRUB-Logic as outlined in Table 2.1.

The same information – i.e. SubStrategies – can be used and reused for all 9 distinct but inter-related stages without needless translations and reiterations of the language used by the various stakeholders in each stage. When stakeholders involved in all 9 of the above steps *speak the same strategy-language (PRUB-Logic)* they can communicate effectively and also inter-link their respective activities.

Types/layers of strategies

The team at OpenStrategies Ltd has found it useful to define three broad categories of strategies (*Validating Strategies*, pages 14–16 and many other pages):

1. Aspirational strategies. These high-level strategies outline the 'big picture' of what needs to be done (Projects) to produce assets (Results) to motivate stakeholders and be used (Uses) to create Global and Motivational Worth (Benefits).
2. Guidance strategies. These mid-level strategies get into enough detail to guide middle management without being totally specific.
3. Operational strategies. These grass-roots-level strategies provide exact details of what needs to be done on a day-to-day basis. They are often called Action Plans

As described in *Validating* Strategies, an overall OpenStrategy in a large, complex, multi-stakeholder environment will contain:

a) a set of Values (see Glossary);
b) a set of Fundamental Principles (essentially 'behaviours') that translate the Values into practical terms which describe what the Values will look like when they are embodied in PRUB-Logic;
c) 1 Aspirational SubStrategy, underpinned by;
d) 10–20 Guidance SubStrategies, each underpinned by;
e) 20 or more Operational SubStrategies.

Table 2.1   The 9 Stages in the OpenStrategies sequence based on PRUB-Logic

Stage description	What this stage will achieve to enable the next stage	Key stakeholders likely to be involved in this stage	What factors will these stakeholders focus on in each stage?
Stage 1: Understand Uses and Benefits	A clear and widely shared understanding of what people want to do, and why	Purchasers, end-users/customers, taxpayers; planners, market researchers, elected officials	What do end-users *really* want to do or be, and *why?*
Stage 2: Understand suppliers' perspectives	A clear and widely shared understanding of what Projects and Results could *potentially* enable and motivate the desired Uses and Benefits	Purchasers; suppliers; single-issue thinkers	What options are there for enabling and motivating the desired Uses and Benefits?
Stage 3: Develop Evidence-based strategies	Many communally owned interlinked and *Validated* SubStrategies which could *potentially* be doable and worth implementing	Planners, strategists, lawyers, communities	Will the SubStrategies definitely work? How do we know? How confident are we? Will the SubStrategies be legal? Who could implement them? Who else could contribute to a SubStrategy?
Stage 4: Validate the strategies by determining their Worth	A set of succinct business cases (*Validated SubStrategies*) which are both Globally and Motivationally Worth it	Accountants, financial planners, business analysts, 'the four well-beings' specialists, advocacy groups	What 'Worth' does each SubStrategy create in terms of all 'four well-beings'? How are the SubStrategies 'Worth it' (both Globally and Motivationally — see chapter 7)? Do sufficient resources even exist to potentially implement each SubStrategy?
Stage 5: Make investment decisions	A list of business cases (*Validated SubStrategies*) which different stakeholders have prioritised (some being universally supported and some supported by sub-groups)	Boards of directors, senior executives, shareholders, elected officials, taxpayers, advocacy groups	What SubStrategies are *most* 'Worth it'? Which SubStrategies are Worth most to which end-users/customers? What is the right mix of 'the four well-beings' for each SubStrategy? How might SubStrategies fit within known budgets?

Stage	Description	Stakeholders	Key Questions
Stage 6: Create performance-based contracts	Various stakeholders are committed to implementing the SubStrategies that they have prioritised	Senior executives, project managers, operational management, staff, citizens	How/when/where/what will actually be created and Used to generate Benefits? Who will be responsible and accountable? How will success be managed?
Stage 7: Implement strategies	Efficiently run Projects have produced effective Results which efficiently enabled and motivated Uses to create effective Benefits	Project managers, operational management, staff, citizens	Have we correctly allocated resources? Are people sufficiently trained? Does everyone know exactly what they need to do?
Stage 8: Performance manage the strategies	Compelling performance Evidence has guided the efficiency of the Projects and Uses to create (respectively) Results and Benefits	Performance management and quality assurance professionals, auditors, project managers, contractors, communities	What does the monitoring and recording of progress tell us? Are things being done efficiently. How should we act on this information?
Stage 9: Review and update the strategies	A continually emerging refined set of *Validated* SubStrategies for more efficiently and effectively enabling and motivating better Uses and Benefits	Boards of directors, senior executives, elected officials, taxpayers	Did it work? Was it effective? What can we learn from what happened? Are our stakeholders happy with us? What can we do better (start again at Stage I)?

Human cognitive limits

SubStrategies based on PRUB-Logic recognise, accept and work within typical human cognitive limits, guided by:

1. Miller's law (http://www.businessdictionary.com/definition/Miller-s-Law.html) which asserts that humans can simultaneously hold 7 +/- -2 interconnected ideas in their heads.

2. we assert that when information is presented diagrammatically, humans can simultaneously handle just 15 +/-5 pieces of information (think back to the last time your eyes glazed over as you tried to understand a diagram with more than 15 pieces of information in it). We call this 'Driver's First Law'.

Because of human's cognitive limitations, each PRUB-Logic-based SubStrategy should contain no more than 15 +/- 5 boxes of information. However, there can be many such SubStrategies in an overall 'OpenStrategy' as described earlier relating to a transport strategy with a hierarchy of *sub*-SubStrategies.

So, the *Validating Strategies* system is based on our core dictum that strategies/plans/funding applications/contracts/performance management must be based on:

> the smallest amount of strategic information that has the highest value to the most stakeholders

Integrating stakeholder information

Strategic actions/business cases/contracts are easier to integrate when they all use the same PRUB-Logic. This integration can be:

1. Vertical: linking Aspirational strategies/contracts down through Guidance strategies/contracts to Operational strategies/contracts.

2. Horizontal: linking strategies/contracts across themes; across different end-user groups; across suppliers; across funders and resource suppliers.

3. Sequential: strategies/contracts that follow each other (e.g. a primary education strategy followed by a secondary education

strategy followed by a tertiary education strategy followed by an employment strategy).

As discussed in detail in *Validating Strategies* it is therefore essential, when establishing a strategy, to determine the scope or the boundaries of the strategy, i.e. its start and finish points. For the example of 3 education strategies followed by an employment strategy, is there a desire for a total of 4, sequential strategies in which the Uses and Benefits in the earlier strategies equate to the Projects and Results in subsequent strategies? Or would it be preferable to have a 3-step education strategy and a single employment strategy, or just one overall education and employment strategy? Establishing the scope of a strategy is a crucially important skill which is included in the 3-day *Validating Strategies* course that is currently certified by the Cologne University of Technology, Science and the Arts (contact the author for details phil@openstrategies.com).

Performance management

PRUB-Logic-based SubStrategies provide a robust platform for accurate performance measurement and management and guide the collection of the *right* information. Performance indicators, targets and measurements (PITMs) are directly 'attached to' Projects, Results, Uses and Benefits. They are not just 'random things that are easy to measure' but are precisely associated with the key elements of SubStrategies, i.e. with the Projects, Results, Uses and Benefits.

A performance 'indicator' is the parameter that will be measured and which will be *useful for managing performance*. The desired value of that indicator is a 'target'. The actual measurement of the indicator is the 'measurement' (*Validating Strategies* Chapter 2 Section 2.10 page 37).

PITMs of Projects and Uses provide information on *Efficiency*.

PITMs of Results and Benefits provide information on *Effectiveness*.

PITMs for Projects and Results are *lead PITMs* and measures of *progress* as they provide early information on the efficiency and effectiveness of SubStrategies.

PITMs for Uses and Benefits are *lag PITMs* and measures of *success* as they provide later-stage information on the efficiency and effectiveness of SubStrategies

Validation

The *Validating Strategies* system insists that strategies be *'Validated'*. This means they must be:

a. Logical: there must be unbroken logical links from Projects through Results and Uses to Benefits.

b. Evidence-based: they must be supported by compelling Evidence that they will actually work, and this means that each and every Link in the PRUB-Logic sequence must be supported by compelling Evidence.

c. Worth it:

    i. they must be 'Globally Worth It': that is, the cumulative net value or Worth of the Benefits to all stakeholders must exceed the sum of the costs of the Projects *plus* the Use costs – where 'Worth' is defined in terms of the 4 well-beings; and

    ii. they must be 'Motivationally Worth It': that is, they must be sufficiently Worthwhile to each stakeholder such that they will each be motivated to make their necessary contributions to implementing the strategy (see Chapter 7 in this book).

In situations where there are a number of ways of achieving the same Benefits, a SubStrategy must be demonstrably the *best* SubStrategy (i.e. the *most* logical and/or the one with the *most* compelling Evidence and/or the one that is *most* Globally and Motivationally Worth-it).

Validating Strategies distinguishes between capital investment (e.g. that are required to establish a service) and operational investment (e.g. that are required to fund an ongoing service). Both types of investment are classified as 'Projects' but capital investments are typically one-off investments whereas operational investments are typically ongoing investments.

In summary, PRUB-Logic underpins and seamlessly links all 9 stages in the sequence:

1. Stage 1 – Understand Uses and Benefits: engage with end-users to determine what they want to do and why (Uses and Benefits).

2.   Stage 2 – Understand Projects and Results: engage with service suppliers to determine what they can potentially provide (Projects and Results).
3.   Stage 3 – Develop Evidence-based strategies: create logical, Evidence-based SubStrategies aligning user requirements with suppliers' insights.
4.   Stage 4 – Validate SubStrategies by determining their Worth: determine both the Global Worth and the Motivational Worth.
5.   Stage 5 – Make investment decisions: compare SubStrategies and select the best ones for investment.
6.   Stage 6 – Develop performance-based contracts: incorporate Validated SubStrategies and performance indicators and targets into robust contracts.
7.   Stage 7 – Implement strategies: Follow the PRUB-sequence to implement strategies
8.   Stage 8 – Performance manage strategies: use measurements of indicators to guide the *Efficient* implementation of current strategies.
9.   Stage 9 – Review and update strategies: review the *Effectiveness* of current strategies and update them where appropriate.

Chapters 4–12 explain these 9 stages and demonstrate how they work using 3 different hypothetical but based-on-fact scenarios:

1.   A large multi-stakeholder strategy to redevelop a suburban central business district after a major natural disaster such as an earthquake.
2.   A large multi-stakeholder strategy to improve the water quality in the Pingo river.
3.   A smaller but still complex strategy to reduce childhood obesity.

But first I need to introduce the principles of PRUB-Accountability in Chapter 3.

Chapter 3

Who is accountable for effectiveness and efficiency?

Accountability: Noun – the state of being accountable, liable or answerable.
Accountable: Adjective – subject to the obligation to report, explain, or justify something; responsible; answerable

This chapter discusses two aspects of accountability:

1. The important distinction between 'accountable for' and 'accountable to'.
2. Who is 'accountable for' different aspects of Projects, Results, Uses and Benefits.

3.1 'Accountable for' and 'accountable to'

The term 'accountability' is commonly used in two ways

1. 'Accountable for' – i.e. being accountable *for* achieving what you said you were going to achieve.
2. 'Accountable to' – i.e. reporting *to* someone about whether you did or didn't achieve what you said you were going to achieve.

The following paragraphs present the case that being 'accountable for' is overwhelmingly more important than being 'accountable to'.

This is so important that in our world of PRUB-Logic we do not allow the concept of 'accountable to' and instead replace it with 'reporting to'.

3.1.1 'BEING ACCOUNTABLE *FOR* ACHIEVING WHAT YOU PROMISED':

a.   This is, in our view, the only meaningful form of accountability

b.   It focuses:

    i.   firstly, on what has been achieved; and

    ii.   only secondly, on who was supposed to achieve it.

c.   It therefore describes concrete facts about whether or not what stakeholders want to be achieved has actually been achieved and this is the overall purpose of strategies, i.e. to *achieve things, especially to enable and motivate Uses to create Benefits.*

d.   If relevant stakeholders have achieved what they set out to achieve then *they have been accountable, whether or not they report on it*

e.   If relevant stakeholders have *not* achieved what they set out to achieve then that is what will matter to most stakeholders. Certainly, most stakeholders will want someone 'held to account' but *the key issue will be that the desired achievements weren't achieved – whether or not they report on it is of secondary importance.*

3.1.2 BEING ACCOUNTABLE *TO* SOMEONE':

a.   It is too easy to claim that someone has 'been accountable' because they have 'been accountable *to*' by sending someone a report or having a meeting with whoever they were 'accountable to', even if they haven't achieved what they promised to achieve (they were not *accountable for*). This is not 'being accountable' – it is merely 'reporting' and it has minimal value relative to the desired achievements.

b.   Because 'being accountable *to*' is seldom well defined and so seldom seems to lead to any significant action for failure to 'be accountable *for*' it is too often pointless. This frequently results in people who do not achieve what they promised to achieve receiving merely a slap on the wrist with a wet bus ticket, while all those stakeholders who were supposed to gain Benefits from what was supposed to be achieved getting nothing.

c.   'Accountable *to*' is therefore frequently an all-too-easy way-out for people who do not achieve what they said they would – they claim 'accountability' because they reported to someone despite failing to achieve.

So, in the world of OpenStrategies we do not allow the concept of 'account-able to'. We use 'accountable for' and 'reporting to'.

We believe this is profoundly important.

3.2   PRUB-Logic Accountability

To be successful, any project, programme or portfolio (3Ps) of work needs to be well governed from start to finish. This means that 'some-one' needs to be responsible for each and every element of the 3Ps and to make sure that each element: is well governed; builds successfully on previous work; and that it contributes effectively to subsequent work or to end-Uses and Benefits (outcomes). This is the principle of PRUB-Logic accountability.

In practice, many people are needed to make accountability work, whether they are customer engagement specialists, strategists/planners, business case developers, decision makers, contract specifiers or project managers. Because the work of all these people needs to be integrated, they need a simple, common language and thinking structure for joint and individual 'accountability'.

This chapter introduces the 'PRUB-Accountability Matrix': a succinct framework for understanding and pragmatically managing accountability.

The following sections clarify PRUB-Logic Accountability by:

1.   Distilling and defining exactly what these accountabilities are
2.   Showing where they arise in the 9 stage OpenStrategies sequence starting with end-user engagement and working through supplier-engagement, strategy development, busi-ness cases, investment decisions, contacts, implementation, performance management and review.
3.   Identifying who is responsible for each type of accountability throughout the above sequence.

3.3   Two types of PRUB-Accountability

There are two types of accountability:

1.   Effectiveness accountability.
2.   Efficiency accountability.

Table 3.1   Effectiveness and Efficiency

Effectiveness	Efficiency
Effectiveness confirms if the *right things have been done*	Efficiency identifies if *things are being done* 'right'
Effectiveness relates to *consequences of actions*, i.e. *what* things were achieved	Efficiency relates to the *actions themselves* i.e. *how* things are being achieved
Effectiveness is determined at a one-off point-in-time at the end of one or more actions i.e. what things *were* achieved. Effectiveness is measured intermittently	Efficiency is determined continuously during one or more actions i.e. how things *are being* achieved. Efficiency can be monitored continuously
Desired effectiveness can be identified before actions are taken but *actual* effectiveness is confirmed only after the actions *have been taken*	*Desired* efficiency can be identified before actions are taken but *actual* efficiency is confirmed only while actions *are underway*

The table above summarises the characteristics of effectiveness and efficiency.

Being accountable for effectiveness is therefore significantly different from being accountable for efficiency.

3.4   Effectiveness

Effectiveness is a measure of the consequence created by an action.

Effectiveness is not a measure of the action itself but rather of the 'things created by the action'. Effectiveness confirms if the *right things were achieved* rather than identifying if *things are being done 'right'* (which is efficiency). So, effectiveness is a measure of things, not a measure of actions. For example, numerous actions might be undertaken to improve the quality of the water in a river. The amount of improvement in the quality of the water (the consequence) is a measure of effectiveness.

Certainly, the effectiveness of a thing created by an action informs whether or not the action was the right action, but it is not the action itself that is at the heart of effectiveness.

Effectiveness is a measure of the *consequences of actions* and not a measure of the actions themselves (efficiency).

Actual effectiveness is fully confirmed *at the end of the action* when 'things' have been created.

Desired effectiveness can be identified *before any action takes place*.

It may be possible to monitor an action to *predict* if effectiveness will be achieved at the end of an action, but the effectiveness itself is the *endpoint* of the action, not the *process* of the action. It may also be possible to have a series of milestones at which the *desired* effectiveness of each step in a multi-step process can be confirmed (or not) as the *actual* effectiveness of the milestone. But the overall effectiveness can be confirmed only at the end of the process when there is 100% clarity that the desired outcomes has been achieved (or not).

Because the full confirmation of effectiveness does not occur until the end of an action, this means that indicators associated with effectiveness tend to be 'lag indicators' in that they provide information that can be acted on only late in any process or action.

3.5   Efficiency

Efficiency is a measure of how well an action is being done.

Efficiency is a measure of processes, not of 'things'. Efficiency determines if *things are being done 'right'* rather than if the *right things were created* (which is effectiveness). So, efficiency is a measure of actions and processes, not a measure of things. If we consider the earlier example of actions to improve the quality of water in a river, then measures of the actions themselves are measures of efficiency. The speed and timeliness of the actions are measures of efficiency. The rate of expenditure on the actions relative to what they are achieving is another measure of efficiency.

Efficiency can be continuously monitored during an action or process as distinct from effectiveness which can only be fully determined at the end of an action or process.

Desired efficiency can be identified *at the start* of a process but *actual* efficiency can only be confirmed *during* a process.

Actual efficiency confirms if processes and actions *are* being done 'right' whereas actual effectiveness confirms if the right things *were* created. So, effectiveness and efficiency management operate on different timescales: efficiency management is continuous whereas effectiveness management is intermittent. Efficiency can *be measured and acted on continuously* during a process or action whereas effectiveness can only *be confirmed at milestones or at the end of an action but can be predicted (with varying degrees of accuracy) and potentially acted on during an action or process.*

Because efficiency is determined during an action or process, this means that indicators associated with efficiency tend to be 'lead indicators' in that they provide information that can be acted on immediately and continually during any process or action.

3.6 Actions required for effectiveness and efficiency

It is all too easy for effectiveness and efficiency accountabilities to remain vague, unattributed and unmanaged, especially in a complex environment with many actions and stakeholders with diverse agendas. Yet it is especially in such complex, multi-stakeholder environments that all stakeholders must understand and be able to collaboratively implement accountabilities. So, they need a common, simple 'accountability framework and language' that will guide them collectively from initial stakeholder engagement right through to implementation, performance management and review.

Accountability for both effectiveness and efficiency involves taking ownership of each type of accountability for each of the following 4 steps:

1. *Identify and Link*: Identify/define the desired effectiveness and efficiency and how they are interlinked (What should effectiveness look like in a given situation? What should efficiency look like in this situation? How should efficiency affect effectiveness?):

  a) Considering the earlier example relating to river water quality, a timely (efficient) action will generate improved water quality (effectiveness) sooner. A low-cost (efficient) action which generates improved water quality will do so cost-effectively.

2. *Value and prioritise*: Decide what is most important to monitor and manage (*which* effectiveness and *which* efficiency are most important? What indicators are relevant? What targets are appropriate?):

  a) For example, are the levels of nitrate in the river water more/less important than the levels of faecal coliforms and if so, how will they be measured and what are the acceptable (target) levels?

3. *Specify*: Document all aspects of efficiency and accountability and how they will be managed and achieved. (How will the prioritised efficiency and effectiveness be monitored and managed?):

  a) What are the target values of water quality? Who will measure them? What test methods will they use? How often will they measure them? What actions will be taken based on the measurement Results? And so on.

4.   *Implement, Performance Manage and confirm*: monitor, manage and confirm effectiveness and efficiency (Monitor, report and take actions to optimise effectiveness and efficiency):

   a)   Take the actions to improve river water quality; monitor how efficiently they are being done; monitor the subsequent water quality; take actions to improve the water quality improvement Projects where appropriate and so on.

So, full accountability includes deciding who is responsible for each of the 4 PRUB-Accountability steps of:

1.   identifying;
2.   valuing/prioritising;
3.   specifying;
4.   implementing/performance-managing/confirming both effectiveness and efficiency.

3.7 Structuring accountability thinking using PRUB-Logic

The following discussion demonstrates how PRUB-Logic provides a robust framework for accountability management.

As shown in Figure 3.1, PRUB represents the sequence:

Projects create **R**esults that enable and motivate **U**ses to create **B**enefits.

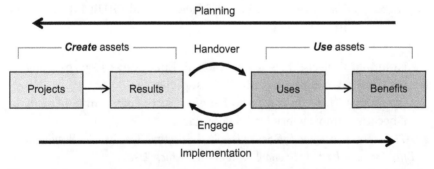

Figure 3.1   **Projects create Results (outputs) that enable and motivate Uses to create Benefits (outcomes).**

Recapping:

- Projects and Uses are actions/processes which should be performed efficiently. Projects can be efficient (or not). Uses can be efficient (or not).
- Results and Benefits are consequences of actions (things) which can be effective or not. A Result can be an effective Result because it is the consequence of the right, efficient Project. The *determination of that effectiveness* is a measure of the Result, not a measure of the Project.
- A Benefit can be an effective Benefit because it is the consequence of the right, efficient Use. The *determination of that effectiveness* is a measure of the Benefit, not a measure of the Use
- So PRUB-Logic identifies 4 types of accountability:
  1.   Accountability for Project-Efficiency.
  2.   Accountability for Result-Effectiveness.
  3.   Accountability for Use-Efficiency.
  4.   Accountability for Benefit-Effectiveness.

This is shown in Figure 3.2:

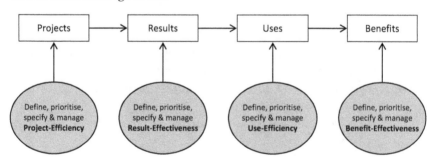

Figure 3.2   The location of PRUB-Efficiency and PRUB-Effectiveness in PRUB-Logic.

Note that Project-Efficiency and Result-Effectiveness can be *managed* because they are under the control of a supplier.

In contrast, Use-Efficiency and Benefit-Effectiveness can only be *influenced* because almost every Use is voluntary.

Therefore, to achieve Efficient Uses and Effective Benefits, the Results must be Effective in order to both enable and motivate their Uses.

So 'Outcomes Accountability' is unequivocally dependent on accountability for Projects, Results and Uses.

As noted above, each of these 4 types of accountability need to be:

1.   identified;
2.   valued and prioritised;
3.   specified;
4.   implemented, performance managed and confirmed.

Each of the four types of accountability and their four associated actions need to be *owned* by someone, giving a matrix of 16 'accountabilities' that need to be understood, owned and managed.

For example, someone needs to be accountable for *identifying* what is meant by Result-Effectiveness within a given action plan. Someone needs to be accountable for *specifying* Benefit-Effectiveness and someone needs to be accountable for *performance-managing* Use-Efficiency and so on.

3.8   Ownership of accountabilities – theory

Who is accountable?

Let us explore a simple scenario in which a government agency (purchaser) wishes to purchase services from a supplier and those services are to service the public (end-users) who the government department represents through the democratic process.

This scenario can be generalised to most purchaser/supplier arrangements.

Purchasers need to be confident that the right, effective Results will be created (Project-Effectiveness), that they will be easy, efficient and motivational to Use (Use-Efficiency) and that these Uses will create the right Benefits (Benefit-Effectiveness).

The purchaser also needs to make sure that these accountabilities will be effectively managed/influenced even if the purchaser cannot actually control that management. For example, the purchaser may *identify, prioritise and specify* a particular level of Project-Efficiency but only the supplier can *manage* Project-Efficiency.

So, the *default* responsibility for the various types of accountability and accountability-actions are as shown in Table 3.2.

Table 3.2shows that the majority of accountabilities, by default, initially sit with purchasers and not with suppliers.

Certainly, purchasers can subcontract some aspects of these accountabilities to suppliers but ultimately the purchasers must ensure that they

Table 3.2 Default accountabilities in the PRUB-Accountability matrix

Accountabilities for Effectiveness and Efficiency (E&E)	Project-Efficiency (running Projects 'right')	Result-Effectiveness (the right Result)	Use-Efficiency (Uses happening 'right')	Benefit-Effectiveness (the right Benefits)
Identify and link desired E&E	Purchasers	Purchasers	Purchasers	Purchasers
Value and prioritise desired E&E	Purchasers	Purchasers	Purchasers	Purchasers
Specify desired E&E	Suppliers + purchasers	Suppliers + purchasers	Purchasers	Purchasers
Implement, Performance-manage and confirm actual E&E	Suppliers	Suppliers	Purchasers	Purchasers

purchase, and are accountable for, the *right and effective* Results, *the right and efficient* Uses and the *right and effective* Benefits.

For example, a purchaser could contract a supplier to engage with end-users to:

1. understand what the users believe are the right Benefits (identifying Benefits-Effectiveness);
2. identify how to make each Use as efficient as possible (identifying Uses-Efficiency);
3. define the most efficient Uses to generate those Benefits (comparing potentially competing Uses-Efficiencies);
4. identify the optimal Results to enable and motivate those Uses (identifying Results-Effectiveness).

The supplier might carry out this engagement and present the purchaser with robust information on Benefits-Effectiveness, Uses-Efficiency and Results-Effectiveness.

But at the end of the day, the purchaser is ultimately accountable for accepting:

1. the right Results from suppliers' Projects;
2. the efficiency of their Uses; and
3. the effectiveness of their Benefits.

Therefore, most aspects of accountability, especially 'outcomes accountability', are by default the primary responsibility of purchasers, not of suppliers.

So, it will be incumbent on the purchaser to make sure that strategies, performance management parameters and accountabilities are reliable enough to act on it.

What does 'reliable enough to act on' mean?

It means that the SubStrategies that will guide the necessary and sufficient actions are *Validated*, i.e. as described in detail in *Validating Strategies* section 2.8 and related sections, specifically:

1. That the Links from Projects to Results to Uses and Benefits are *logical*.
2. That there is compelling cause-and-effect Evidence that a Project *will* produce the desired Results; that the Results *will* be Used; and that the Uses *will* create the desired Benefits.

3.   That the consolidated Worth of all the Benefits is greater than the combined costs of all the Projects *plus* the costs of all the Uses (Global Worth) and that each and every stakeholder is gaining sufficiently Worthwhile Benefits from the strategy to motivate them to play their part (Motivational Worth).

While a supplier might carry out the task of identifying these three accountabilities and may do so in a very robust and credible manner, the *purchaser remains accountable for accepting and basing investment decisions on that information.*

Of particular importance is the different nature of accountability for Projects/Results and Uses/Benefits.

Because Projects/Results are generally within the domain of one or more suppliers, they can usually be *managed*. This applies both to Projects that produce Results that enable and motivate Uses and also to internal Projects that produce 'Adoptable Orphan Results' (see *Validating Strategies*, section 2.15) that get Adopted into further internal Projects which in turn create Results that get Used.

In contrast, because Uses/Benefits are usually outside the domain of any organisation, they can generally only be *influenced*. Most Uses are voluntary so they cannot be *managed*, they can only be *influenced*.

This means that the desired Uses and Benefits will only happen (voluntarily) if the *right* Results are readily available. This in turn means that accountability for Uses and Benefits is inherently different from accountability for Projects and Results because Uses/Benefits-accountabilities are dependent on effective accountability for Results and Projects to produce the *right* Results. So even though the desire might be to focus on 'outcomes-based accountability', such accountability is necessarily and unequivocally dependent on Projects-Efficiency, Results-Effectiveness and Uses-Efficiency.

3.9 Ownership of accountabilities – worked example

Let's explore what this means for just 4 out of 16 accountability elements of a hypothetical strategy to improve river water quality in the Pingo River.

1.   *Identify* Benefits-Effectiveness: Someone needs to determine what 'good river water quality' means. Does it include a full spectrum of factors (nitrates, coliforms, bacteria, turbidity, suspended solids, salinity, chemical composition, temperature) or just one or more of these parameters?

2.   *Identify* Uses-Efficiency: How will the various Uses of the water happen? Will it be used for swimming? Wading? Fishing? By fish and their food sources? By birds and insects? For irrigation? For boating? Other?

3.   *Value and prioritise* desired Uses-Efficiency: Which Uses will be most efficient: human Uses? fish Uses? bird Uses? other?

4.   *Specify* desired Projects-Efficiency; Results-Effectiveness; Uses-Efficiency; and Benefits-Effectiveness: Agree on what will be monitored, who will monitor it and what actions will be taken in response to the monitoring data?

In practice, this could look like the following:

1.   The purchaser is territorial local authority (LTA-A) which is responsible, on behalf of its voters, for developing, implementing and policing strategies on water quality management in rivers and catchments.

2.   The suppliers are a number of organisations who take actions to improve water quality: These could be:

   a.   landowners or industry who plant riparian strips or reduce their discharge of contaminants to minimise nutrient run-off;

   b.   earthmoving companies who realign a river, perhaps re-introducing a more natural meandering route for a river that had previously been straightened by drainage engineers, or who may make localised river-beaches for swimming, or who engineer modified flows so as to improve fish habitats;

   c.   a second territorial local authority (TLA-B) who is responsible for road transport and implementing better controls on run-off from roads into rivers;

   d.   environmental groups who may act in both a supplier role (planting riparian strips on public land) and as users (walking alongside, fishing in and boating on the river);

   e.   minority groups, especially those who may not be well represented;

   f.   science and technology companies who specialise in monitoring environmental parameters and recommending scientifically valid management solutions.

They may work directly for the purchaser or indirectly for the purchaser by working directly for the earth moving company;

g.   and others.

3.   End-users could be the environment itself (fish, invertebrates, birds, insects, plants); swimmers, fishermen, boaties, walkers, members of environmental groups, school children, pets and others.

Even in this relatively straightforward example of improving the quality of water in a single river there are many stakeholders, many actions that need to be taken, many end-users and many desired and often competing Benefits. It is complex, with a lot of uncertainty about the diverse information needing to be found, shared, understood, and acted on.

All the stakeholders (except the fish …) need to understand and play their part to achieve the desired Benefits. And someone needs to represent the fish and advocate for them.

It is therefore essential to have a simple, transparent and effective system for agreeing:

1.   What needs to be achieved (Effectiveness of Results and Benefits).
2.   How it needs to be done (Efficiency of Projects and Uses).
3.   Who will be responsible (accountability) for each of the four steps in managing effectiveness and efficiency: identification; valuing and prioritising; specifying; implementing and performance-managing.

Table 3.3 shows how accountabilities *might hypothetically but reasonably* be assigned for the river water quality project using a PRUB-Accountability matrix.

3.10   Accountabilities in practice

Figure 3.3 shows the accountabilities of each of the 9 stages of the OpenStrategies system.

Figure 3.3 identifies the sequencing as to when various accountabilities and accountability-actions need to be considered.

Table 3.3 Possible accountabilities for a river water quality improvement programme as defined by the PRUB-Accountability matrix

Accountabilities for Effectiveness and Efficiency (E&E)	Project-Efficiency (running Projects 'right')	Result-Effectiveness (the right Result)	Use-Efficiency (Uses happening 'right')	Benefit-Effectiveness (the right Benefits)
Identify and link desired E&E	P: Determined by TLA-A through discussions with suppliers and through scientific research	P: Determined by TLA-A in discussions with all the suppliers	P: Determined by the TLA-A via subcontracts to recreational and environmental groups	P: Determined by TLA-A via subcontracts to environmental groups
Value and prioritise desired E&E	P: Prioritised by TLA-A through discussions with suppliers and taxpayers	P: Prioritised by TLA-A through discussions with taxpayers and recreational and environmental groups	P: Prioritised by TLA-A through discussions with recreational and environmental groups	P: Prioritised by TLA-A through discussions with recreational and environmental groups
Specify desired E&E	S+P: Specified collaboratively by TLA-A and suppliers	S+P: Specified collaboratively by TLA-A and suppliers	P: Specified by TLA-A copy-pasting above information into contracts	P: Specified by TLA-A copy-pasting above information into contracts
Implement, performance-manage and confirm actual E&E	S: Achieved primarily by suppliers who may have subcontracts with each other	S: Achieved primarily by suppliers who may have subcontracts with each other	P: Monitored by TLA-A who may negotiate modified specifications and contracts with suppliers	P: Monitored by TLA-A who may negotiate modified specifications and contracts with suppliers

Note: (P = Purchasers; S = Suppliers).

Stage	Accountabilities for this Stage
1. Understand Uses and Benefits: What do users want to do (Uses) and why (Benefits)?	Identify Benefit-Effectiveness (P) & Use-Efficiency (P)
2. Understand Projects and Results: What can suppliers create (Results)	Identify Result-Effectiveness (P) & Project-Efficiency (P)
3. Develop Evidence-based Strategies: Links Projects & Results to Uses & Benefits	Convincingly Link Result-Effectiveness to Use-Efficiency & Benefit-Effectiveness (P)
4. Validate strategies by determining their Global & Motivational Worths	Quantify value/significance of Project-Efficiency (P); Result-Effectiveness (P); Use-Efficiency (P); Benefit-Effectiveness (P)
5. Make investment decisions: Compare SubStrategies & select the best ones	Prioritise Project-Efficiency (P); Result-Effectiveness (P); Use-Efficiency (P); Benefits-Effectiveness (P)
6. Create performance-based contracts: Create contracts based on SubStrategies	Specify/negotiate Project-Efficiency (P/S); Result-Effectiveness (P/S); Use-Efficiency (P); Benefit-Effectiveness (P)
7. Implement strategies: Projects create Results & enable Uses to create Benefits	Efficiently run Projects (S) to produce Effective Results (S) which will be Efficiently Used (P) to create Effective Benefits (P)
8. Manage performance: *Manage* Projects → Results: *Influence* Uses → Benefits	Monitor & Manage Project-Efficiency & Result-Effectiveness (S): Monitor & *Influence* Use-Efficiency & Benefit-Effectiveness (P)
9. Review & update strategies: Improve Projects to create better Results, Uses & Benefits	Update Projects(S) to produce more Effectives Results (P), more Efficient Uses (P) & more Effective Benefits (P)

Figure 3.3 *Default* effectiveness and efficiency accountabilities as they relate to developing and implementing strategies and contracts. These accountabilities may be subcontracted to other parties. (P = Purchasers; S = Suppliers).

These accountabilities and actions can be considered linearly, as shown in Figure 3.3, and this aligns with what is known as the waterfall approach to project and programme management (https://en.wikipedia.org/wiki/Waterfall_model).

These accountabilities and actions can also be carried out iteratively, so that for example, Steps 1 and 2 (engaging with end-users and suppliers) may be repeated a number of times before a particular sequence of Projects-Results-Uses-Benefits is agreed on. This iterative approach aligns with Agile methodologies (Agile) (https://www.apm.org.uk/resources/find-a-resource/agile-project-management/). For example, the purpose of Agile's method of rapid prototyping is to identify the minimal viable product (an adequate Result) and subsequently to build on that to create a more robust and viable product. This means that Agile needs to find out what Projects will produce the right Results that people will be motivated to Use to create their desired Benefits.

But instead of conducting focus groups or sending out questionnaires to determine end-users' needs, Agile determines users' needs by repeatedly asking end-users to Use and provide feedback on possible Results (prototypes). This feedback is then used to rapidly improve and repeat the prototyping Projects to produce better prototype Results that increasingly enable and motivate end-users' Uses to create Benefits. Eventually a prototype will emerge from Agile that confirms the *effectiveness of the final prototype (Result)* to enable and motivate the desired Uses and Benefits.

Recapping:

PRUB-Logic confirms that there are no shortcuts from inputs (Projects) to outcomes (Benefits). To be successful, implementation of a strategy/contract *must* follow the sequence: *"Projects create Results that enable and motivate Uses to create Benefits"*.

Crucially, *only Uses create Benefits*. Suppliers *never* create Benefits/outcomes. Suppliers can only *influence*, not *ensure* Uses and Benefits.

Suppliers can:

1. *Manage/Ensure* Results:
    a. *Ensure* that they are proposing and achieving the *right* Results (Result-Effectiveness-accountability).
    b. *Ensure* that they are creating the right Results in the *right way* (Project-Efficiency-accountability)
2. *Influence* Benefits. This *influence* can be strong *provided the strategically right Results/services are being provided* (Result-Effectiveness accountability). This is why contracts and

services must be underpinned by *Validated* strategies which in turn are guided by effective prior engagement with all affected stakeholders.

Commissioners and suppliers therefore need to conclusively demonstrate, in their strategies, investment decisions and in their services, that they will create the *right Results* so that users will genuinely use the services and that these Uses will genuinely create the desired outcomes/Benefits.

3.11   Accountability conclusions

Being *Accountable for* is much more meaningful and valuable than being *Accountable to*. This is so important that in our world of PRUB-Logic we no longer use the term 'accountable to' but replace it with 'reporting to'.
   Unless negotiated otherwise:

1.   Purchasers are *primarily* accountable for Result-Effectiveness and Benefit-Effectiveness
2.   Purchasers are *primarily* accountable for Use-Efficiency.
3.   Suppliers are *primarily* accountable for Project-Efficiency.

This is in stark contrast with how accountabilities are often attributed – in which suppliers far too regularly get landed with the whole lot, sometimes even retrospectively towards the end of a programme of work. In reality, *purchasers are responsible for most accountabilities* and their associated actions. In many instances, purchasers may negotiate with suppliers and others for a different sharing of accountabilities, but at the end of the day the purchaser is ultimately accountable for making sure that:

1.   The *right* Benefits are created (Benefits-Effectiveness).
2.   The Uses are efficient (Uses-Efficiency).
3.   And therefore, that the *right* Results are created (Results-Effectiveness).

The next 9 chapters discuss and demonstrate the 9 stages of the OpenStrategies system and processes.

Chapter 4

Stage 1 – Understand Uses and Benefits

Reminder: Our purpose is to *enable and motivate Uses to create Benefits*
PRUB Mantra #1: *Only Uses create Benefits*

What is Stage 1?

Stage 1 in the OpenStrategies system consists of engaging with end-users in various ways in order to accurately understand what they want to *do* (Uses) and *why* they want to do them (Benefits).

Ideally, the method of engagement will be in a format the suits the end-users. The engagement may be one-off or iterative. It may consist of, for example, focus groups, questionnaires, repeated Agile-style pro-totyping and end-user testing; phone or web-based survey, discussions with end-users or some of the many other methods of engagement. The purpose in all cases must be to understand what users want to *do* (Uses) and *why* (Benefits) so that these Uses and Benefits *influence* the design and selection of Projects and Results.

This book focuses on the *content* of the engagement questions (what users want to do and why) and not on the *method* of engagement.

Crucially, distinction must be made between users and Uses. Just because there are users does not mean that they will undertake the *intended* Uses. For example, the construction of a swimming pool may have been justified by the expectation that users would Use the swim-ming pool to swim lengths and so create the Benefit of 'physically and mentally healthier users'. In reality, the users may have turned up at the pool as expected but their Use may be primarily 'floating around having conversations with their friends'. This is unlikely to generate the desired Benefit of 'physically and mentally healthier users' although it may create a Benefit of 'stronger social cohesion'.

So *the existence of users does not guarantee that the intended Uses must happen.* Hence the criticality of Stage 1 to compellingly determine what *Uses* genuinely will happen, not just which *users* will turn up.

This section will emphasise what this stage will and must achieve in order to enable the next stage because no stage has any value in isolation from the other stages. The outputs from an engagement process must be Adopted and used to guide strategies so the engagement process must produce outputs (Orphan Results) which will definitely be Adopted by subsequent stages.

So, Stage 1 produces detailed information on Uses and Benefits and these must *influence* the design and selection of Projects and Results. This means that in the arena of 'change management', it is generally the Uses that must influence the Results/Projects rather than the 'change managers' trying to change the Uses and Benefits.

So, perhaps controversially, project managers/purchasers are often the stakeholders who need to be 'change managed', not the users.

What Stage 1 will achieve in order to support the other 8 stages

1.   Essential: Stage 1 will generate a thorough (objective, quantified, verified) and documented understanding of what end-users will *actually do* (Uses) and *why* (Benefits). These Uses and Benefits could be proposed new Uses and Benefits to create a new strategy or existing Uses and Benefits which are being audited to improve an existing strategy. All subsequent 8 stages are critically dependent on this information being precise and accurate. Stage 1 is shown in context in Figure 4.1.

2.   Optional: Stage 1 may also document what end-users believe they need (a *necessary and sufficient set* of Results) in order to enable and motivate their Uses.

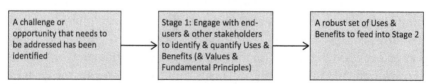

A challenge or opportunity that needs to be addressed has been identified	Stage 1: Engage with end-users & other stakeholders to identify & quantify Uses & Benefits (& Values & Fundamental Principles)	A robust set of Uses & Benefits to feed into Stage 2

Figure 4.1   **The precursor to Stage 1, Stage 1 itself and what Stage 1 must feed into Stage 2.**

WHY IS STAGE I IMPORTANT?

1. To be effective, all subsequent 8 stages depend on the thorough understanding of Uses and Benefits because all 8 stages are designed *to enable and motivate Uses to create Benefits.*

2. The Uses dictate what Results or combination of Results may be both *necessary and sufficient* to enable and motivate the Uses to create Benefits.

3. Benefits *emerge* from Uses but *only* if the Uses occur due to the right Results being in place. The right Results will only be created if they are guided by an accurate understanding of Uses, Benefits and the Worths of those Benefits. So, Benefits cannot be *realised* by project managers if the wrong Projects are being run. In reality if the right Projects are producing the right Results then Uses and Benefits will *emerge* without needing to be *realised* or *managed* at the end of the implementation process.

4. So 'Benefits Realisation/Management' must start right at the beginning of any ideas-to-implementation process so as to enable Benefits to *emerge* from Uses, rather than being something that project managers and others somehow 'realise/manage' towards the end of the process.

5. The Benefits, and the Worth of the Benefits to those receiving the Benefits, identify the *motivations* for the Uses by end-users. So, Benefits and their Worths must be *actual* Benefits with *actual* Worths *as perceived by the users* and not *hypothetical* Benefits and Worths that are *hoped-for* by purchasers and suppliers. This is crucially important, so I repeat: Benefits, and the Worth of the Benefits, identify the *motivations* for the Uses by end-users. If end-users are not motivated to undertake the Uses, then they will not happen and the Benefits will not be created. End-user motivation is crucial to the successful implementation of strategies.

6. Many people love to propose solutions before a problem has been defined or before end-user requirements have been objectively identified. Many stakeholders (end-users, purchasers and suppliers) will too-quickly jump to conclusions about what Results are 'obviously' needed to address a problem or opportunity, but over and over again these 'obvious answers' are wrong.

   "There is always a well-known solution to every human problem – neat, plausible, and wrong" (Mencken H.L. (1921). Prejudices: Second Series. London: University of Toronto)

Stage I is therefore essential for focusing all stakeholders' minds on determining the *actual* Uses and Benefits/Motivations of end-users that really will happen and not just their assumed or desired or wished-for Uses and Benefits.

SUMMARY OF THE START-TO-FINISH
ACTION SEQUENCE FOR STAGE I

Stage 1 requires the following actions as are explained in more detail below:

1.   Determine and agree on the problem/opportunity.
2.   Determine and agree on Values (See *Validating Strategies*, page 192).
3.   Determine and agree on Fundamental Principles which correlate with those Values (see *Validating Strategies*, page 200).
4.   Determine what users want to *do* (Uses) and *why* (Benefits and Motivations) and collate their answers as a set of *potential* Uses and Benefits and their Worths.
5.   Optionally: determine what products/services/infrastructure (i.e. Results) users think they need to enable and motivate them to do the Uses to obtain the Benefits. Where possible, start collecting cause-and-effect Evidence that Results *will* genuinely be Used and that these Uses *will* generate the Benefits.
6.   Add performance indicators as narratives associated with each box of information i.e. what will success look like for each Benefit, Use and Result?
7.   Cross-check that the desired Uses and Benefits align with the agreed Values and Fundamental Principles.
8.   Ask other stakeholders how the potential Results and Uses will affect them and where appropriate add these effects into the emerging SubStrategy.

Explanation of the start-to-finish
action sequence for Stage I

1.   Determine and agree on the problem/opportunity
   a.   Too often an engagement process is stated as seeking to understand what end-users 'want' which implies that whoever is running the engagement intends to find ways of meeting some or all of those wants. This builds unrealistic expectations in the minds of the end-users. In reality it is frequently the case that whoever

is running the engagement has a completely different agenda. In a recent example in Christchurch NZ, the entity running the engagement actually wanted to create a 'spatial plan' for an area – which was essential-to-have – but it was not about 'wants', even though the engagement process itself asked residents about their 'wants'. Where this is the case it is essential to clarify for the end-users what will/will not be in the scope of the engagement and the extent to which the end-users' perspectives will genuinely influence investment decisions.

b. End-users should play a major role in defining the problem/opportunity. This is because end-users almost always pay for 100% of whatever is produced, either through taxes, local government rates or through their payment for commercial services. There is no such thing as 'government money' or 'local government money' – in reality it is all taxpayers' and ratepayers' and citizens' money which is being managed on behalf of the end-users. Governments and their agencies are generally elected or appointed to represent end-users and therefore they frequently take a leading role in end-user engagement. Often their end-user engagements are not for the purpose of *enabling and motivating Uses to create Benefits* but instead are constrained by a more limited legislative need to do things like: 'create an annual plan'; 'create a 10-year plan'; 'create a spatial plan'; 'create a Master Plan'.

c. Similarly, organisations that run end-user engagement processes often limit their focus to only those actions that *they* can take i.e. it is about defining only those Results that the particular organisation can create themselves. These actions alone may be insufficient to *enable and motivate Uses to create Benefits*. This hugely constrains the engagement because very often other stakeholders are perfectly able to take complementary actions which collectively will produce a full suite of desired necessary and sufficient set of Results that will *enable and motivate Uses to create Benefits*.

d. Ideally, users' identification of their desired Results should come after an initial focus on Uses and Benefits. This is because the Results must unequivo-cally be precisely that complete set of necessary and sufficient Results that will *enable and motivate the Uses to create Benefits*. If these Uses and Benefits are not known and understood it is absolutely impossible to accurately identify the necessary and sufficient set of Results that will enable and motivate unknown Uses. However, pragmatically many stakeholders will want to start their conversations with their ideas about Results and Projects and will not be able to discuss Uses and Benefits until they have unloaded their ideas out of their heads (see *Validating Strategies*, Chapter 5 "Working with Stakeholders").

e. So the challenge or opportunity needs to be clearly defined and scoped right at the start of the process so that all potential beneficiaries of the challenge/oppor-tunity and all potential stakeholders who can contrib-ute are crystal clear on the purpose of the engagement and subsequent strategies and actions right at the beginning of the 9- stage process.

f. In determining the scope of a strategy, it is essential to agree on the start and finish points of the strat-egy. For example, is an 'Education Strategy' going to be a 'Primary Education Strategy' or a 'Secondary Education Strategy' or a 'Tertiary Education Strategy' or a combination of all 3? The Benefits emerging from a Primary Education Strategy would become use-able Results in a Secondary Education Strategy and would become Adoptable Orphan Results in a Tertiary Education Strategy (see *Validating Strategies*, Chapter 7 for important details on establishing the scope of an OpenStrategy).

2. Determine and agree on Values:

a. Values provide high-level guidance on the character-istics of the outcomes/Benefits stakeholders wish to achieve. They do not define the Benefits themselves but rather the *characteristics* of those Benefits. For example, commonly expressed Values (loosely worded here because that is how they are often proposed) include: safety; respect for each other; diversity; thriving; respect for the environment; vibrant; sustainable; clean-green; pure; profitable; sheltered; protected; mentally and physically healthy; equality and equity; collaboration/cooperation; accessible and so on. These terms do not define Benefits or outcomes – they *characterise* outcomes/Benefits

b.   Stakeholders will readily offer such Values but they are frequently loosely worded and need to be pinned down as to exactly what they mean. They need to be translated into true Values and agreed by all stakeholders as being the right Values correctly phrased for all the stakeholders. For example 'equality' is already a Value but 'vibrant' (an adjective) would need to be translated into a true Value such as 'cultural vibrancy' or 'vibrant biodiversity'

c.   Each Value needs to be accompanied by an explanation of what end-users think it means.

d.   Certain Values tend to emerge in many different strategies. For example, most of the Values listed in 2a above would apply to most urban strategies. So, although Values are important, they provide only minimal direction as to what should happen, and why, within any specific strategy.

e.   Not all stakeholders need to share all the Values – this is not *yet* (!) the time for a conversation to prioritise competing Values.

f.   Note that Values (more akin to beliefs) are not the same as 'value' (the Worth of something, especially of Benefits). This is why in the world of OpenStrategies we no longer refer to the 'value' of Benefits because this is too often confused with Values. Instead, we refer to the 'Worth' of Benefits as discussed in more detail in Stage 4 (Chapter 7).

3.   Determine and agree on Fundamental Principles which correlate with those Values:

a.   Fundamental Principles are primarily *rules* that reflect *how* Values will be addressed. For example, a Value like 'transparency' might lead to a Fundamental Principle that: "end-user engagement will be open to all and all documentation will be publically and freely available". This does not define outcomes or Benefits but it does guide *how* Projects and Uses will lead to Uses and Benefits.

b.   A Value of 'collaboration' might translate into a Fundamental Principle of: "all stakeholders have equal speaking rights during end-user engagement" and/or "all Project plans will contain open invitations to other stakeholders to contribute". This is not a Project or an action but a *way of doing things*.

c.   An indigenous community Value such as 'alpine river water represents blood whereas lowland river water represents waste' might generate a Fundamental Principle such as 'we will not mix alpine and lowland waters'. Again, this is not an action but is a way of doing things.

4.   Determine what users want to *do* (Uses) and *why* (Benefits and Motivations) and collate their answers as a set of *potential* Uses and Benefits and their Worths:

a.   Whatever your engagement process may be, the purpose must be to identify Uses and Benefits. To do this, the best questions to ask over and over again are:

i.   "what do you *want* to *do* and what *will* you *do*?" (Uses);

ii.   "*why* do you want to do these things?" (Benefits). (see *Validating Strategies*, pages 25, 87)

b.   It is important that people tell you what *they want to do*, not what they think *other people ought to do*. We have repeatedly had people tell us they want a cycleway, but on further questioning it turns out that they want to drive to work because there will be less congestion because *everyone else* is using the cycleway. It is very easy to speculate on what other people might want to do or ought to do but such answers are frequently misleading. Your stakeholders are likely to find it challenging to accurately identify what they personally *want* to *do*, and *will do*, and *why*, but it is essential to persist with your questioning because understanding

Uses and Benefits is absolutely fundamental to all subsequent stages.

c.   When you know what people want to do, then ask: "how do you want to do these things? how often? when? where? what are you prepared to pay for doing these things?"

d.   A big challenge in Stage 1 is to keep stakeholders focused on Uses and Benefits because just about everyone is far more comfortable talking about Projects and Results, even before the Uses and Benefits have been identified! If this is allowed to happen it runs a high risk of subsequently producing Orphan Results (*Validating Strategies,* pages 44, 45), i.e. unwanted Results that are futilely looking for Uses. When Uses and Benefits are identified first, they guide the identification of the *right, necessary and sufficient set of* Results that *will* be used.

e.   You will experience people shifting their conversations away from Uses and Benefits to talk about Results. For example, in a hypothetical scenario of the redevelopment of a city centre, Results are likely to be proposed such as "we need more parking" or "the buildings should be designed to have environmentally attractive street frontages". These may be good ideas, but until Uses and Benefits have been accurately defined and *Validated* there can be no confidence that these Results-ideas are the *right* ones for the city centre. So, keep bringing the conversations back to the topic of Uses and Benefits until these have been well defined and then let the conversation move onto Results and Projects.

f.   The question of 'who gets the Benefits' is crucially important because Projects are often promoted which will ultimately lead to Benefits accruing to certain stakeholders when the Projects are actually funded by other stakeholders. Classically, commercial stakeholders frequently propose Projects like stadiums; concert venues; new roads; parking; that they want taxpayers to pay for even though the commercial stakeholders will be the primary financial beneficiaries of the Projects. This is not necessarily a problem as long as all stakeholders are aware of what is going on and give their approval. Perhaps the commercial stakeholders can identify ways in which their desired initiatives can create Benefits for other stakeholders, thereby increasing the chances that their initiatives will be well supported.

g.   Be precise about what the Benefits are, how valuable the Benefits are *to the end-users*, and who gets any of the other Benefits, for example, operators of stadiums; retailers who Benefit from new roads and parking and so on. This is important information because it indicates who might reasonably be expected to contribute funding and resources to the Projects and who should reasonably be included in future discussions. It also helps identify *who* will be motivated and *how* they will each be motivated (by Benefits *to them*).

h.   It is useful to start determining the net Worths (see Chapter 7 where, importantly, we distinguish 'Worths' from 'Values') of the Benefits and who determines the Worths. It is generally not reasonable for stakeholders to determine the Worths of Benefits to *other* stakeholders. Those who get the Benefits should be the ones who determine the Worths of Benefits *to them*. Suppliers or purchasers may also receive Benefits and it is similarly appropriate for them to determine the Worth of Benefits to them. For example, a stadium may generate Benefits to end-users who attend sports events with their local teams (a Benefit could perhaps be: 'a sense of local community cohesion from having attended the game with fellow citizens') and also enjoy eating hot-dogs. This same Use also generates Benefits (profits) to commercial operators who sell hot-dogs at those games.

i.   Make the emerging ideas as visible to as many end-users as possible (subject to commercial confidentialities) because often stakeholders can build on each other's ideas.

j.   Recapping: it is essential to identify *Benefits to end-users* plus *Benefits to other stakeholders* (see bullet-point 9 below about identifying 'dis-Benefits' to stakeholders).

k.   Then insert the Uses and Benefits into the two right-hand columns of a draft SubStrategy. At this point there may be dozens or more Uses and Benefits, so it is likely to be helpful to cluster Uses and Benefits into categories, each with its own draft SubStrategy (see the example demonstrated below).

5.   Optionally: determine what products/services/infrastructure (i.e. Results) users think they need to enable and motivate them to do the Uses and obtain the Benefits. We make this stage optional because once Uses and Benefits have been accurately identified, many of the necessary Results are obvious. However, as noted above, stakeholders often want to talk about Projects and Results before discussing Uses and Benefits. It is OK to let this happen for a short period until the stakeholders have had their say, to acknowledge their contributions and to then 'park them' (e.g. on a whiteboard) so they will not be forgotten and then move on to identifying Uses and Benefits:

a.   While many of the *physical* Results required to enable the identified Uses will now be obvious to most stakeholders it is nevertheless essential in Stage 2 below to *Validate* the proposed Results with compelling *cause-and-effect Evidence* that:

i.   the Results *really will* be Used;

ii.   the Uses of the Results *really will* create the desired Benefits;

iii.   the Results are the *best* Results.

b.   While most of the *necessary* Results will be obvious now that the Uses and Benefits are understood, this does not mean that these Results are automatically *sufficient* as well as *necessary*. For example, one crucial factor that is often overlooked is the *marketing* of those Results to end-users so that they:

i.   know about the Results;

ii.   are motivated to use the Results.

c.   Then insert the proposed Results into the emerging SubStrategy(ies) as a set of *potential* Results, each linked to its appropriate Uses and Benefits.

d.   See Stage 2 for a more detailed discussion of Projects and Results.

6.   Where possible, start collecting cause-and-effect Evidence that Results *will* be Used and that these Uses *will* generate the Benefits:

   a.   At this stage, users will make many claims about their intended Uses of Results. It is essential in Stage 3 below that these claims be *Validated* with compelling cause-and-effect Evidence that these Uses really will happen at the levels that end-users say they will. The above cycleway example (people saying they want a cycleway but later admitting that they won't actually use it) is a classic example of this problem.

   b.   So, although the *Validation* of such Evidence is part of Stage 3, it is always worthwhile to collect as much cause-and-effect Evidence as possible at this initial stage of engagement with end-users.

   c.   In our experience, *the most important cause-and-effect-Evidence is that which confirms that Results really will be Used*. It may be difficult to get such Evidence initially, other than end-users earnestly saying they really will Use the Results, but it is imperative that Evidence be found and *Validated* before Projects are initiated to create the proposed Results, Uses and Benefits. Generally there will be *some* Evidence available, for example regional/national data, market research information, the results of pilots or trials, overseas precedents and so on.

   d.   Cause-and-effect Evidence relates to actions causing things. Therefore cause-and-effect Evidence relates to Projects causing Results and Uses causing Benefits.

7.   Add performance indicators as narratives associated with each box of information i.e. what will success look like for each Benefit, Use and Result?

   a.   Performance indicators need to be confirmed in later stages, but as with Evidence, it is worthwhile collecting *end-users'* perspectives on key performance indicators during this initial engagement process.

   b.   Performance indicators must be things that can be measured: by size; by number; by frequency; by speed;

by cost; by desirability; by colour; by timing; by accessibility; by ease of use and so on.

c.   End-users need to tell you what success will look like *to them*. Part of this success will be captured in the definition of the Benefits (e.g. 'healthy citizens') and Uses but performance indicators get into more detail e.g. *"how many* people will be *how* healthy?"; "how many people say they will purchase goods in the rejuvenated central business district (CBD) and *how much* will they *actually* spend?"; "what actions will obese people and diabetics *actually* take to improve their health (as distinct from the actions that health professionals believe they *ought* to take)?"; "what are the measures of a healthy ecosystem?" and so on.

d.   What end-users define as success may come as a surprise, so it is important to hear their views. For example, while the indicator of a desired Benefit of young people exercising in a gym complex might be 'the number of young people who are healthier', that may not be a key performance indicator for young people. Instead, young people might say that their desired Benefit is "I know more young people of the opposite sex" with their key performance indicator being "I am now in a relationship". So, the *motivation* for the young people relates to relationships, with 'health' as an un-sought-after but nice-to-have side-effect. So, if an agency wants to improve the health of young people by providing a gym complex then it will be important that the gym environment offers opportunities for young people to socialise as well as exercise so as to tap into the *motivation* of the young people (see Stage 8 Chapter 11).

e.   Performance indicators can relate both to actions (Projects and Uses) and to consequences of actions (Results and Benefits).

f.   A performance indicator is the 'thing' that will be measured. The desired value of that indicator is a 'target'. The actual measurement of the indicator is the 'measurement' (*Validating Strategies*, Chapter 2 section 2.10 page 37).

8.   Cross-check that the desired Uses and Benefits align with the agreed Values and Fundamental Principles

   a.   As strategies evolve, original Values and Fundamental Principles often become modified as various stakeholders' priorities change. It is important to check that the desired Uses and Benefits still align with the evolving Values and Fundamental Principles of *all* stakeholders and not just those of one or two dominant stakeholders.

   b.   Because financial factors are generally either easier to measure or are more immediately compelling, there is a risk that strategies which had broad 'well-being' intentions at the start morph into primarily financially-driven strategies, putting a lower Worth on the other three well-beings (social, environmental, cultural). This may happen despite the fact that the Values espoused by many stakeholder groups tend to place a lot of emphasis on non-commercial well-beings.

   c.   In public-sector strategies there are frequently passionate advocates for various courses of action whether they are commercial, social, environmental or cultural. They are likely to assertively propose various courses of action which may or may not align with the overall Values and Fundamental Principles of the full stakeholder group.

   d.   Are there any stakeholders who are not represented in the engagement process? Are there 'silent stakeholders' such as minority groups or unborn children and the environment which cannot speak for themselves? If so then at this stage it is important to check that *their* Values, Uses and Benefits have been taken into account. For example, with the environment will animals, birds, insects, fish, plants and the environment in general thrive if the proposed Uses and Benefits (and their necessary Results) happen?

   e.   Where there is misalignment two options are possible, either: the Values and Fundamental Principles are both updated to reflect the emerging Uses and Benefits; and/or the Uses and Benefits are updated to reflect the Values and Fundamental Principles.

9.   Ask other stakeholders how the potential Results and Uses will affect them and where appropriate add these effects into the emerging SubStrategy:

   a.   Many initiatives impact positively or negatively on more than the intended users and beneficiaries. For example, a new rail link from London to Birmingham would impact heavily on landowners along the rail corridor as well as on birds and animals in the area. If the impact has been on the environment, has the 'environment's own perspectives' been fully considered? Interestingly, in New Zealand, the Whanganui River has now been officially given the status of a person with its own team of people legally representing and advocating for its interests.

   b.   So, at this early stage in the 9-stage OpenStrategies process, it is important to check who else might be affected (positively or negatively) by the emerging Results, Uses and Benefits because such effects may be significant enough to totally derail the strategy. Alternatively, such unintended consequences may be positive and so help justify implementing the strategy. Either way the full effects of a strategy on all possible stakeholders needs to be at least identified, if not quantified, in this Stage 1.

Demonstration of Stage I actions

Stage 1 will now be demonstrated using the example of the redevelopment of a declining CBD in a major suburb in a city.

1.   What is the problem?

   a.   A major suburban CBD has been damaged by a natural disaster (e.g. an earthquake or flood) which has made the area largely unusable for several years. Many historical customers for the area have migrated their shopping, use of commercial services and recreation to other parts of the city. Now that the main clean-up of the area has been completed, the suburban CBD business and land owners, locals, local and central government, community groups and others want to develop and implement a strategy to rejuvenate the local CBD and its nearby surrounds.

b.   This is necessarily a gross oversimplification of the situation as there will be a great many constraints (budgets; who are the decision makers; legislation; timeframes; planning restrictions etc) but it nevertheless provides an example to demonstrate the process of engagement to obtain accurate information on Uses and Benefits.

2.   Determine and agree on the Values for the area:

a.   Stakeholders will readily offer Values for such an area and they will tend to be similar for many different CBDs around the world. Common Values that are likely to be proposed include loosely worded concepts such as safety, thriving, environmentally healthy, vibrant, sustainable, clean-green, pure, profitable, sheltered, culturally safe and community oriented. These are all nice-to-haves and they are useful for checking if the subsequent strategy is appropriate. An example of a loosely worded Value translated into a true Value and accompanied by a definition of its meaning *by the end-users* might be:

i.   proposed 'Value' = 'vibrant';

ii.   actual Value = 'vibrancy';

ii.   definition of vibrancy as defined by end-users = "the CBD is full of people obtaining goods and services with a significant number also having fun, especially at weekends" (which actually defines 'vibrant' – but that's probably good enough for most purposes. Much as we like to be pedantic with our PRUB-Logic, we can compromise on something like this).

3.   Determine and agree on Fundamental Principles which correlate with those Values:

a.   A Value such as 'safety' might be represented by a Fundamental Principle such as: "motor vehicle speeds will be restricted in the CBD to create a pedestrian-friendly space" which in turn might translate into a Use of: "vehicles are driving slowly due to rigidly enforced speed limits and speed-limiting road humps".

b.   A Value such as 'environmentally healthy' might be represented by a Fundamental Principle such as: "emissions into the air will be better than World Health Organisation standards". This in turn might translate into a Result such as: "Regulations prohibit diesel-powered vehicles in the local CBD".

c.   A Value such as 'sheltered' might be represented by a Fundamental Principle that: "shelter will be provided primarily through good design rather than through post-construction add-ons". This in turn could lead to a rule (a Result) that "most streets will run north-south at right angles to a prevailing cold easterly wind, with minimal connecting east-west streets".

4.   Determine what users want to *do* and *why*:

a.   The following start of a SubStrategy (see Figure 4.2) identifies *some* of the key Uses and Benefits that might reasonably emerge from engagement with end-users who have an interest in a rejuvenated suburban CBD. It is likely that in a real CBD-regeneration strategy that very many more Uses and Benefits will emerge but the example below is indicative of what happens when end-users are invited to say what they want to *do* (Uses) and *why* (Benefits)

b.   Note the wide range of Uses with equally wide-ranging financial, environmental, cultural and social Benefits, all of which provide motivation for various stakeholders to make the strategy work.

5.   Determine what products/services/infrastructure (i.e. Results) users think they need to enable and motivate them to do the Uses and obtain the Benefits. Insert their answers into the emerging SubStrategy as a set of *potential* Results, each linked to its appropriate Uses and Benefits:

a.   Notice how obvious most of the *necessary* Results are now that the Uses and Benefits are understood. This does not mean that these Results are automatically *sufficient* as well as *necessary* but it is a good start.

b.   The emerging hypothetical SubStrategy now looks like Figure 4.3.

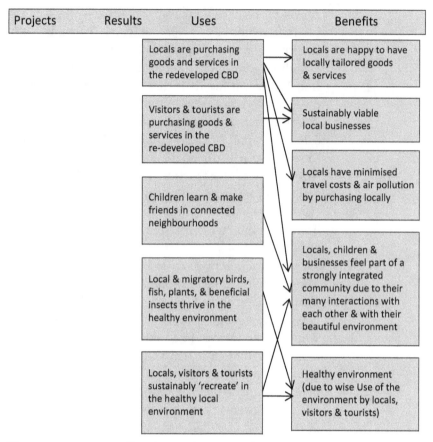

| Projects | Results | Uses | Benefits |

Figure 4.2 **A small subset of Uses and Benefits for the hypothetical redevelopment of a CBD that has been badly damaged by a natural disaster such as an earthquake.**

6.   Where possible, collect cause-and-effect Evidence that Uses *will* generate the Benefits and that Results *will* be Used:

a.   Enthusiastic locals who want to see the CBD regenerated are likely to offer optimistic assertions about their likely future Uses of the CBD. Further, they are likely to extrapolate those optimistic Uses to other stakeholders. In Stage 3, this Evidence needs to be *Validated* before it can be relied on. Types of Evidence might include precedents, market research in a wider population, results of pilot projects and so on

b.   Some of the best Evidence for a regenerating CBD might relate to what happened in the CBD prior to the

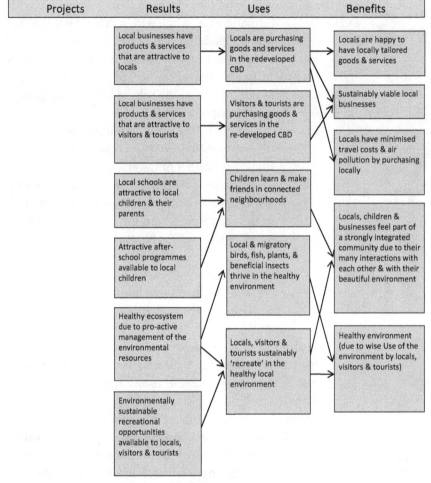

Figure 4.3   Hypothetical Results, Uses and Benefits for the redevelopment of a declining CBD.

disaster i.e. how many local people spent how much how often in the old CBD? How many non-locals spent how much how often in the old CBD?

c.   Market research with a wider and more representative end-user base should always supplement opt-in engagement where the data is genuinely unavailable through other sources.

d.   Other Evidence may come from other similarly regenerating CBDs in comparable suburbs elsewhere in the country or overseas.

7. Add performance indicators as narratives associated with each box of information i.e. what will success look like for each Benefit, Use and Result?

    a. Examples of performance indicators that end-users may identify for a regenerating CBD might be:

        i. 'the number of shops selling interesting goods' (an indicator of a Result);

        ii. 'the number of people who will purchase goods in the rejuvenated CBD and how much they will spend?' (indicators of Uses);

        iii. 'the levels of turnover that business owners need to have in order to be sustainable and pay rent to landowners?' (an indicator of a Benefit);

        iv. 'the measures of a healthy ecosystem?' (an indicator of *both* a Result and a Benefit – see *Validating Strategies*, page 128 for a discussion of how a healthy environment can be both a Result and a Benefit depending on how it came about).

    b. In this Stage 1, the primary focus will be on performance indicators for Uses and Benefits, with performance indicators for Projects and Results emerging in Stage 2.

    c. Performance indicators of Benefits (and, to a lesser extent, indicators of Uses) provide convincing information about the *success* of SubStrategy implementation. In contrast, performance indicators for Projects and Results are early measures of the *progress* of implementing a SubStrategy; *they are not measures of success!*

8. Cross-check that the desired Uses and Benefits align with the originally agreed Values and Fundamental Principles (or with updated Values and Fundamental Principles):

    a. A rejuvenated CBD must either be financially viable or be supported by subsidies, so financial well-being will be a 'given'.

    b. Financial viability is therefore necessary but probably not sufficient to create a 'thriving, sustainable, vibrant, environmentally healthy and safe' CBD.

    c. Because the success of the CBD will depend heavily on end-users frequenting the area and supporting commercial and retail businesses, if these end-users are motivated strongly by non-financial as well as financial factors then the CBD will need to be 'environmentally healthy' and 'culturally safe' and 'community oriented'.

d.   Further, the views of 'silent stakeholders' such as the environment cannot speak for themselves so their own Uses and Benefits must be taken into account.

e.   In this example, financial well-being *depends on* social, environmental and cultural well-being *and vice versa*. Therefore to be successful, implementation of the emergent rejuvenation strategy needs to performance-manage indicators of all four well-beings. Note however that in almost every instance, well-beings cannot be *managed* – they can only be *influenced* by providing the *right* Results to *enable and motivate Uses to create Benefits*.

9. Ask other stakeholders how the potential Results and Uses will affect them and where appropriate add these effects into the emerging SubStrategy

a.   A revamped CBD will impact positively or negatively on nearby residents, tourists, the transport system, the water and waste-water system, the energy system, the environment, schools, disabled people and so on.

b.   Check that all possibly affected stakeholders' needs (their own Uses and Benefits) have been adequately considered, for example: will the presence of a new supermarket and outlet for alcohol, cigarettes and fast food have an impact on the health of local school children? Will the realigned north-south streets (to create more sheltered areas) impede some stakeholders whose primary direction of travel is east-west? How will the commercial success of the rejuvenated CBD impact on small traders in nearby areas of the suburb? And so on.

c.   Many minorities will not engage spontaneously/voluntarily so this may require specific targeting of these stakeholders in proportion to the level of commitment to ensuring that the rejuvenation genuinely Benefits all stakeholders.

Accountabilities in Stage I

Stage 1:

1. *Identifies:* Uses-Efficiencies and Benefits-Effectiveness and starts identifying Results-Effectiveness.
2. *Responsibilities:* Identifying and defining (as distinct from *delivering)* Benefits-Effectiveness and Results-Effectiveness and Uses-Efficiency are *primarily* the responsibility of purchasers, with much of the information sourced from end-users who also have some responsibility to define their Uses and Benefits. The purchasers may choose to subcontract this identification step to suppliers and others.

Comments

1. So that all stakeholders understand each other it is important that everyone speaks the same language. This is why we use PRUB-Logic as it encapsulates: *"the **smallest amount** of strategic information that has the **highest value** to the **most** stakeholders".*
2. The distinction between 'users' and 'Uses' is critically important. The existence of users does not create Benefits! You can have thousands of users but if they do not do the Uses then the intended Benefits may not be created. It is the *actions* (i.e. the *Uses*) of users that create the Benefits. This reinforces the importance of being confident that the *Uses will actually happen* as distinct from knowing that there *are many **potential** users but no confidence that they will undertake the Uses.*
3. In order to *enable and motivate Uses to create Benefits* we must know with maximum possible confidence exactly what Uses will *actually happen* and not just the Uses that 'we' would *like* to happen or believe *should* happen or which we fondly imagine *might* happen. If Uses do not happen, then Benefits will not be created. So, Stage 1 is crucial for underpinning all of the following 8 stages for creating and implementing a strategy.
4. ***Crucially*** ... Stage 1 is the most difficult of the 9 OpenStrategies stages because it generally requires widespread engagement with diverse groups of end-users who will almost invariably

want to tell you what they 'want to *have*' (Results) and may struggle to identify what they 'want to *do* and *why*' (Uses and Benefits).

5.   Why is this? Results are external to the User so are less personal than Uses which are very much internal in their personal space. Users do not need to take much responsibility for *wanting/requesting* Results (usually from *other* stakeholders) but they do need to take responsibility for *actually doing* Uses.

6.   Unfortunately, it is easier for stakeholders to allocate responsibility (i.e. for providing Results) to someone else than to accept responsibility for themselves (i.e. for Uses and Benefits). This is why identifying Uses and Benefits is so challenging yet essential for underpinning successful strategies.

7.   We have also found that people find it easy to propose Uses that *other people should do* but find it more difficult to define Uses that *'we should do ourselves'*.

8.   Because Stage 1 is right at the beginning of the 9-stage process, in many situations very little will already have been rigorously defined, so conversations will ideally, indeed necessarily, be open-ended and exploratory. In other situations, there will be rigorous constraints on what is possible, so in such cases conversations would need to be similarly constrained, with clear explanations about those constraints.

9.   Many stakeholders will struggle with this degree of uncertainty and leap in with their 'solutions' even before the challenges and opportunities have been fully defined. Many stakeholders (end-users, purchasers and suppliers) will too-quickly jump to conclusions about what Results are 'obviously' needed to address a challenge or opportunity, but over and over again these 'obvious answers' are not optimal. It is Worth repeating Mencken's dictum:

> There is always a well-known solution to every
> human problem - neat, plausible, and wrong.

10.   It is therefore imperative to keep asking 'Use-oriented' questions until you *know without doubt* what the desired Uses and Benefits *actually* are and which *really will* happen and hence what Results are *likely* to be the right ones and users will be *motivated* to Use them.

11.   Purchasers, in particular, often start their stakeholder engagement processes with strong preconceptions of what Results are needed to enable end-users to do what they want to do. It is essential that purchasers keep an open mind in Stage 1 because their beliefs will almost certainly be challenged by the on the ground reality of end-users' experiences and wishes. So a key purpose of end-user engagement is to discover/check/validate all perspectives and beliefs.

12.   It is therefore essential to remember the mantra that *'only Uses create Benefits'* and that because such Uses are almost always voluntary, they will only happen if users have the motivation and resources (including the *right* Results) to make them happen. So, the PRUB-Logic approach is in stark contrast to the 'build it and they will come' approach.

13.   The Results need to be the *right* Results *plus* end-users need to easily find out about them, to find them straightforward to Use (or be trained in their Uses) and be motivated to Use them. This means that many SubStrategies need to contain Projects and Results that: inform end-users; make the Results user-friendly; and train/motivate/incentivise end-users.

14.   Our experience of engagement with thousands of stakeholders shows that it is almost always helpful to ask stakeholders to 'take off their organisational hats and become citizens' for the duration of the engagement so that they focus on *what* needs to be done and *why*, and not on *who* needs to do Projects. If stakeholders introduce their organisational biases too soon in the process they often constrain thinking along the lines of "*we* cannot do that so it cannot be part of the strategy". In reality, it is frequently the case that *a different stakeholder* can in fact 'do that thing', often unexpectedly so. So, we recommend that when running engagements you invite people to: "give your name and your topics of interest but *do not tell us your role or which organisation you represent*". This helps people get into a mindset of being open-minded contributors to a strategy development *thinking* process, free of organisational constraints. Certainly once the strategic ideas have been translated into *Validated Strategies*, the various stakeholders can reassume their organisational responsibilities and advise which SubStrategies they can contribute to and how – indeed this is essential.

15. Purchasers and suppliers cannot justifiably blame end-users if they do not use the Results that have been provided to create the desired Benefits. In such situations, the purchasers and suppliers must take responsibility (be accountable) for having provided the *wrong Results* due to not having fully understood end-users' *actual* desired Uses and Benefits.

16. There are many traditional methods of obtaining information from end-users but most of them focus on asking end-users what they *want* to have (Results) rather than what they want to *do (Uses) and why (Benefits)*. There is nothing wrong with the methods *per se*, it is just that they need to focus on questions about Uses, not questions about Results. The PRUB-Logic approach sits comfortably within all common engagement and research methods for obtaining robust information about end-users' needs and wants.

17. Irrespective of which method is used to engage with end-users, the *purpose* of these methods is the same in every case: to fully understand and to *verify* end-users Uses and Benefits i.e. if the proposed Results are made available, will they *actually* be Used at the levels indicated and will they *actually* generate the desired Benefits?

18. Without this verification (see the next 2 stages), all subsequent 8 stages in the OpenStrategies system will be severely weakened because they will not know what they are trying to achieve – i.e. *'to enable and motivate Uses to create Benefits'*.

Once you have collected and are confident about *actual* Uses and Benefits as defined by end-users then you are ready to move to Stage 2 – Understand Projects and Results (Chapter 5).

Chapter 5

Stage 2 – Understand Projects and Results

Reminder: Our purpose is *to enable and motivate Uses to create Benefits*
PRUB Mantra #1: *Only Uses create Benefits*
PRUB Mantra #2: Uses need the *right* Results or they won't happen

What is Stage 2?

Stage 2 will identify potential Projects and Results that will *enable and motivate Uses and Benefits.*

Stage 2 consists of:

1.   engaging with suppliers and purchasers to learn how they believe they can create plausible Results that will *enable and motivate Uses to create Benefits.*

What Stage 2 will achieve in order to support the other 8 stages

1.   Stage 2 will produce a list of Projects which suppliers and other stakeholders *could* potentially undertake, which *will* produce Results which are necessary, sufficient and sufficiently attractive to end-users that they *will* be enabled and motivated to Use them to create Benefits. The Results could be products, services or infrastructure.

2.   In this stage, these Results and their Projects can be only loosely linked to the desired Uses and Benefits prior to rigorous Evidence-based linking in Stage 3: Evidence-based Strategies.

3.   These Projects and Results could be proposed and/or existing Projects and Results to create a new strategy or to examine/audit an existing strategy (see Figure 5.1).

WHY IS STAGE 2 IMPORTANT?

1. Because suppliers have often worked with similar end-user groups, they frequently have many good ideas about how to *enable and motivate the Uses and Benefits* identified by the end-users, so their ideas are valuable.

2. Suppliers often also have good ideas about alternative but equally or more effective Results that may enable *the same or different* Uses and Benefits. For example, before Ford supplied the Model T, customers thought they wanted faster horses. Ford's cars enabled them to get to more distant places faster.

3. Suppliers often have fixed ideas about Projects and Results that may not necessarily enable and motivate Uses so it is essential to maintain a focus on *actual* Uses and Benefits *as defined by the end-users* and not just *hypothetical Uses and Benefits desired by suppliers*. The counter-argument also applies: that suppliers *may* have a better understanding of *actual* Uses than end-users due to their experiences elsewhere. The key point is that proposed Projects and Results must correlate with forecast *actual* Uses and Benefits.

4. Many different stakeholders can perform the role of 'suppliers' including end-users themselves. Ideally, a wide range of potential suppliers needs to be consulted because they may come up with unexpected options which end-users and purchasers may not even have thought of.

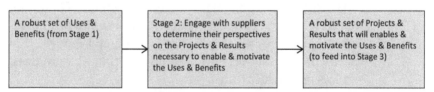

| A robust set of Uses & Benefits (from Stage 1) | Stage 2: Engage with suppliers to determine their perspectives on the Projects & Results necessary to enable & motivate the Uses & Benefits | A robust set of Projects & Results that will enables & motivate the Uses & Benefits (to feed into Stage 3) |

Figure 5.1   **The precursor to Stage 2, Stage 2 itself and what Stage 2 must feed into Stage 3.**

Summary of the start-to-finish action sequence for Stage 2

1.   Start Stage 2 by sharing with all potential suppliers and purchasers the information from Stage 1:
   a.   Values and Fundamental Principles;
   b.   the Uses and Benefits *as defined by the end-users;*
   c.   indications of what end-users believe they need (necessary and sufficient Results) in order to enable and motivate their Uses to create Benefits.
2.   Facilitate suppliers to identify potential Projects that will produce the right set of necessary and sufficient Results that will enable and motivate the previously identified Uses to create Benefits.
3.   Invite suppliers to offer alternative Results that might enable the same Uses and Benefits but also which might *enable and motivate different but equally Worthwhile Uses and Benefits.*
4.   Link the Projects and Results to the Uses and Benefits including to any new Uses and Benefits that night be enabled. In doing so, look for potential negative impacts of the Results and Uses on other Benefits.
5.   Identify and if possible collect cause-and-effect Evidence that would compellingly support the linking of the potential Projects and Results to the desired and/or new Uses and Benefits.
6.   Identify performance indicators which can subsequently be used to monitor and *manage* the Projects and to *influence* the Uses.
7.   Cross-check that the desired Projects, Results, Uses and Benefits still align with the agreed and prioritised Values and Fundamental Principles.

Explanation of the start-to-finish action sequence for Stage 2

1.   Start Stage 2 by selecting suppliers, purchasers and other stakeholders who could reasonably run or contribute to Projects to produce Results that will *enable and motivate the*

Uses to create Benefits as defined by end-users in Stage 1. Share with all potential suppliers and purchasers the information generated in Stage 1:

a.   Values and Fundamental Principles;

b.   the Uses and Benefits *as defined by the end-users;*

c.   indications of what end-users believe they need (Results) in order to enable and motivate their Uses.

Suppliers and purchasers often have fixed ideas about what they want to 'deliver to' end-users so they sometimes struggle to fully hear what end-users want to do and why. While their enthusiastic proposing of their own ideas is welcomed, it is nevertheless essential when engaging with suppliers to keep the initial focus on *actual* Uses and Benefits *as defined by the end-users.* Suppliers need to be guided to explore in some depth exactly what the end-users have said they want to do, and why (i.e. the Benefits that will motivate them do to the Uses) and also to develop an understanding of the Values and Fundamental Principles that must apply to all Projects, Results, Uses and Benefits.

At this point it will be worth checking whether or not a full spectrum of suppliers has been involved, not just the obvious ones but also those who might offer creative solutions

2.   Facilitate suppliers to identify the right (both necessary and sufficient) Results that will 'enable and motivate the previously identified Uses to create Benefits and then to identify the appropriate Projects (Results first, then Projects):

a.   Suppliers generally freely contribute a range of possible Projects and Results to enable and motivate the Uses so it is worth encouraging this conversation to flow freely and to capture as many ideas as possible (they can be *Validated* in Stage 3 below).

b.   Keep the focus first on Results and then on Projects, not the other way around. The risk of starting with Projects is that proponents of the Projects may be so wedded to their Projects that they attempt to make their Results 'fit' the Uses or imagined Uses, rather than letting the Uses guide the Results and Projects so that they are truly fit for purpose. However, also acknowledge that some Project-focused people will have some good ideas so at this early stage in the process, let these ideas emerge because they will be subject to rigorous scrutiny for 'cause-and-effect Evidence' in Stage 3 and for 'Worth' in Stage 4.

c.   Be open to creative ideas. For example, if the Use = 'people are swimming' then appropriate Results could be any of the following: a safe swimming pool; a safely swimmable river; a safely swimmable beach; a safely swimmable harbour; a safely swimmable lake. Each such Result requires a completely different Project from the others. The right Result will emerge from a detailed understanding of the Uses and Benefits.

d.   Do not let apparent resource-limitations stifle the generation of ideas for Results and Projects at this early stage. Often Projects can be run much more cost effectively by some stakeholders than by other stakeholders. For example, in New Zealand the Department of Conservation would have to spend a lot of money to remove wilding pine trees. However, members of tramping and climbing clubs regularly donate their time to cut down the trees for minimal net cost while providing some good healthy outdoor activities for the club members. In this case, the end-users of the environment became the voluntary suppliers of services (Projects) to create an improved environment (Result) that they could hike and climb in (Uses).

e.   With each proposed Result, ask penetrating questions about:

   i.   how will end-users be motivated to Use the Results? (the answer = 'Benefits');

   ii.   how will the end-users learn about the Result? (this identifies possible additional Results);

   iii. will the Result be readily accessible to all end-users? (this identifies possible additional Results);

   iv.   will end-users need training in how to Use the Result? (this identifies possible additional Results).

f.   Add new Projects to address the answers to these questions, for example:

    i.   add a market-research Project to determine more compellingly what will motivate users to Use the Results;

    ii.   add marketing Projects to tell end-users about the Results;

    iii.   change the availability or characteristics of the Results to make them more accessible;

    iv.   develop and disseminate training so that users can easily Use the Results;

g.   Make the lists of emerging Results and Projects as visible to as many stakeholders as possible (subject to commercial confidentialities) so that stakeholders can build on each other's ideas;

h.   In order to enable and motivate Uses, Results must be both necessary and sufficient. If we consider the example of a Result = a swimming pool, then in Stage 2 it is essential to ensure that all the following factors are considered when determining if the set of Results is a *sufficient* set of Results:

    i.   the Results must physically exist (e.g. a swimming pool);

    ii.   the main Result may need to be supported by other physical Results (e.g. car parking and bus stops near the swimming pool);

    iii.   the physical Results may need to be supported by skilled practitioners (e.g. lifeguards, pool maintenance technicians);

    iv.   users need to know about the Results (e.g. via the media);

    v.   users need to comprehend the Results (e.g. to understand the rules of using the swimming pool);

    vi.   users need to access the Results (e.g. by walking, by bus, by bike and by car and the associated physical Results);

    vii.   users need to afford the Results (e.g. the cost of entry *plus* the cost of getting to the pool);

      viii.   users need to know how to use the Results (e.g. when/how they can use the pool in various ways including whether or not they need to be able to swim).

      ix.   users need to be motivated by the Worth of the Benefits they gain (e.g. to cool down on a hot day) from using the Results.

      x.   Only when the set of Results addresses *all* the above bullet points is the set of Results both necessary and sufficient.

3.   Once you have a set of the *right, necessary and sufficient* Results and their associated Projects you can encourage suppliers to then offer different Results that might enable and motivate the same Uses and/or different but equally Worthwhile Uses and Benefits. Suppliers often have alternative ideas on what can be done to enable Uses so it is essential to hear their perspectives. Focus first on the proposed creative Results before defining Projects and consider the need to market the Results, improve their accessibility and provide training if required.

4.   Correlate Projects and Results with the Uses and Benefits:

    a.   Create draft SubStrategies linking Projects and Results to Uses and Benefits. These SubStrategies may grow to be quite large and beyond the cognitive ability of stakeholders to understand them (i.e. beyond 15 +/– 5 Projects, Results, Uses and Benefits). Do not be too concerned at this stage as the most important thing is to capture the ideas. They can be refined into more succinct SubStrategies, or interlinked sets of SubStrategies once all the ideas have been captured.

    b.   In this Stage 2 it is worthwhile to draw on the suppliers' wisdom to at least *correlate* the PRUB Links to determine which Projects *could* create Results which *could* be used and which *could* create Benefits. Stage 3 will subsequently add cause-and-effect Evidence to justify the Links from Projects to Results, Uses and Benefits.

    c.   So, at this point the *logic* (P-R-U-B correlations) of the SubStrategy is coming together, even if that logic has not yet been fully *Validated* by cause-and-effect Evidence.

d.   It often happens at this point that new Uses emerge from the proposed Results. For example, a Result of 'a swimmable river' (due to a Project to eliminate sources of pollution) may open up a new Use of 'people catching fish in the newly cleaned river'. So, although the 9-Stage process is described in this book in a linear fashion, it is frequently worth revisiting earlier stages if subsequent stages unearth new and relevant ideas: which could be positive or negative.

e.   Nothing happens in isolation so even the best SubStrategies will have unintended and sometimes undesirable consequences. For example, a Result of 'more trout in a river' and hence 'better fishing experiences' for end-users might have a negative impact on 'the number of native fish in the river' given the predatory nature of trout. So, Stage 2 is an ideal time to look for and address unintended consequences of Results and Uses.

5.   Identify and if possible collect cause-and-effect Evidence that would compellingly support the linking of the potential Projects and Results to the desired Uses and Benefits:

a.   Although Stage 3 will rigorously collect such cause-and-effect Evidence and add it to the emerging SubStrategies, it is worthwhile to tap into suppliers' wisdom to capture what cause-and-effect Evidence they have readily available.

b.   In our experiences, *the most important cause-and-effect-Evidence is that which confirms that Results really will be Used* because, also in our experience, most strategies fail because Uses do not happen as expected. It may be difficult to get such Evidence initially, other than end-users earnestly saying they really will Use the Results. However, it is imperative that Evidence be found and verified (Stage 3) before Projects are initiated to create the proposed Results to enable and motivate the Uses to create Benefits.

c.   In Stage 2, Project proponents will make claims about how their intended Projects will definitely produce the intended Results which will in turn be Used.

These claims need to be recorded ready for verifying in Stage 3.

d.   Project managers are likely to have a high degree of confidence that their Projects will definitely produce the desired Results because they can *control* their Projects.

e.   In contrast, claims that Uses will definitely follow Results should be verified (Stage 3) before they are accepted because *most Uses cannot be controlled – they can only be influenced by providing the right, necessary and sufficient Results* (see Figure 5.2).

f.   Cause-and-effect Evidence relates to actions causing things. Therefore cause-and-effect Evidence relates to Projects causing Results and Uses causing Benefits.

g.   Evidence can come from many sources such as: successful similar SubStrategies being implemented elsewhere; historical successful SubStrategies; stakeholders' strong commitments to the SubStrategy; changing motivations in end-users due to the impact of social media, empirical data sources including market research and so on.

6.   Identify performance indicators which can subsequently be used to monitor and manage the Projects:

a.   Performance indicators need to be confirmed in later stages, but as with Evidence, it is worthwhile to collect suppliers' perspectives on key performance indicators during this initial engagement process.

b.   Performance indicators must be things that can be measured: by size; by number; by frequency; by speed; by cost; by desirability; by colour; by timing; by accessibility and so on.

c.   In Stage 1, end-users will have already told you what success will look like *to them* and such success will relate primarily to Uses and Benefits.

d.   In Stage 2, suppliers define what success will look like to *them* and such success will relate primarily to Projects and Results. However, for those suppliers who provide an ongoing service, success will also relate to Uses (e.g. how many people Use the service) and the sustainability that arises from those Uses (e.g. profits).

7. Cross-check that the desired Projects and Results and their enabled Uses and Benefits align or suitably balance the agreed Values and Fundamental Principles:

   a. In their enthusiasm to contribute ideas about Projects and Results, suppliers sometimes lose sight of the Values and Fundamental Principles of a specific SubStrategy as they are so keen to 'sell' their particular services into the SubStrategy. This enthusiasm is to be welcomed but must also be tempered by rechecking that their proposals align with the Values and Fundamental Principles.

   b. Frequently, social, cultural and environmental Values are subsumed by financial values in this stage, and indeed in many of the other stages. It is therefore imperative to keep referring back to the full set of Values and Fundamental Principles to ensure that they are *all* given due recognition.

   c. At this stage it may be necessary to revise the Projects/Results/Uses/Benefits or to change the Values and Fundamental Principles. In either case it is essential to involve all affected stakeholders in such revisions. As ideas on proposed Projects, Results, Uses and Benefits emerge, the stakeholders' different perspective on Values and Fundamental Principles are likely to come into stark contrast because the PRUBs clarify what the Values and Fundamental Principles *will look like in practice.* This can be challenging but also highly informative, so this is the ideal trigger to resolve differences (or agree to differ) before getting any further into the 9-stage process.

Demonstration of Stage 2 actions

Stage 2 will now be demonstrated using an example of a SubStrategy on the public health topic of childhood obesity. In this hypothetical example, end-users (children) and their caregivers and other adults in their lives generated the small set of Uses and Benefits in Stage 1 as shown in Figure 5.2. This is just a small subset of the possible Uses and Benefits that could arise in a comprehensive childhood obesity strategy and is provided

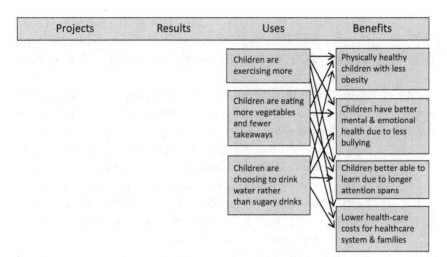

Figure 5.2   Hypothetical Uses and Benefits for SubStrategy on child-hood obesity.

to demonstrate the PRUB-Logic thinking process (starting with Uses and Benefits) rather than attempting to demonstrate a full-scale SubStrategy.

In this example, almost every Use contributes to every Benefit, thereby confirming the interdependent nature of all the actions that need to be taken collaboratively to effectively reduce obesity:

1.   A key point to note is that the children are the users. Only the children can undertake the Uses to achieve the Benefits. So, no matter how inspired and motivated parents and teachers and others there may be, if the children are not motivated to take exercise and consume good food and drink, the Benefits will not arise. This 'motivation' could be voluntary (for example, the children choosing to eat healthy foods because they like them) or less voluntary (children having to eat healthy foods because that is all that is available).

2.   The Uses and Benefits in this example SubStrategy may or may not be valid. They have been proposed by some of those con-sulted in Stage 1 but that does not automatically make them valid or meaningful. The suggestion that the way to minimise bullying by helping children eat and exercise well in order to lose weight would reasonably be seen by many as blaming the victims, rather than targeting the bullies. The key point is that the PRUB-Logic structure brings these issues clearly to

the surface so they can be addressed. In this example it may trigger the development of a separate SubStrategy on bullying and so refocus the obesity strategy on health and away from bullying.

3.   Stage 2 would start by selecting suppliers and other stake-holders who could contribute to Projects that would enable the three Uses identified above and they would then gener-ate Projects and Results to enable and motivate those Uses. In the real world, this SubStrategy would involve many stake-holders including local authorities; the Department of Health; hospitals; primary care medics; the Department of education; sporting clubs; teachers; suppliers of food and other services to schools; parents and the children.

4.   Because there would be a large number of such Projects and Results in this SubStrategy, in this chapter we will focus on gen-erating Results and Projects for just one of the Uses: "Children are choosing to drink water rather than sugary drinks". This initial focus on one Use at a time is typically what happens as Projects and Results are added to SubStrategies. So, a good rule of thumb is to work with one Use at a time and this often leads to a separate (but interlinked) SubStrategy for each Use:

a.   The suppliers would first be shown the set of Values and Fundamental Principles that were generated by the end-users and their representatives (not shown here but they could include concepts relating to health, choice, wisdom, self-esteem, non-bullying and so on).

b.   Then the suppliers would be shown the Uses and Benefits and, in this example, asked to come up with Projects and Results that would lead to the Use of "Children are *choosing* to drink water rather than sug-ary drinks".

c.   A key factor here is the concept of children *choosing* to drink water. Will they be motivated to do this in order to reduce health-system costs or to help themselves learn? Unlikely! One Benefit that might motivate them to drink water is to reduce bullying of overweight children because that has a profound impact on their well-being, but this impact would be delayed so may not be sufficiently motivational in the short term. So, what *would* motivate children to drink water instead of sugar-drinks? Parents, teachers, caregivers, paediatric researchers and the children themselves will have some answers so *ask them*. This example demonstrates the importance of understanding the *motivation for the Uses by the users*.

5.   Facilitate suppliers to identify potential Projects that will produce the right necessary and sufficient Results that will 'enable and motivate the previously identified Uses to create Benefits':

    a.   In this hypothetical example of children *choosing* to drink water, the suppliers (parents; teachers; health specialists and others) came up with the following Results (and Projects for 2 of them) which they believe will *enable and motivate the Uses to create Benefits* (see Figure 5.3).

    b.   In this example, the Projects and Results relate to only one of the Uses. In practice, a series of interlinked SubStrategies would be required to fully address

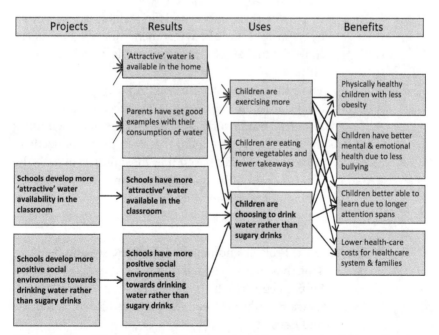

Figure 5.3   Hypothetical Projects, Results, Uses and Benefits for a childhood obesity SubStrategy.

childhood obesity as hinted at by the non-connected clusters of small arrows.

c.   Each of the Results has both a physical element (water) and a motivational element ('attractive'; 'good example'; 'positive social environments') because both the physical and the motivational elements will be required to motivate children to voluntarily drink water. In practice, the terms 'attractive' and 'good example' and 'positive social environments' would need to be defined in some detail to make sure that, for example, the water was genuinely attractive to children and not just attractive to adults.

6.   Invite suppliers to offer different Results that might enable the same and/or different but equally Worthwhile Uses and Benefits:

a.   Suppliers might propose new Results such as "after-school programmes and sports clubs have and promote 'attractive' drinking water".

b.   Other suppliers might propose anti-bullying programmes so that children who are drinking water as part of their efforts to lose weight are supported by a 'positive social environment' and the bullies are trained/educated so that they are less inclined to be bullies.

c.   The PRUB-Logic structure with its emphasis on *enabling and motivating Uses* inserts these proposals into a logical framework and, in this instance, identifies the sobering requirement that each proposal needs to *influence the choices (Uses)* that the children make – the children cannot be *compelled* to drink water. So, there is no point proposing Results that may work for adults if they won't *motivate children to choose water. Only Uses create Benefits!*

7.   Correlate the Projects and Results with the Uses and Benefits:

a.   This has already been done in the above partial SubStrategy in which there are simple and straightforward Links between the proposed Projects, Results and Uses.

b.   In many situations, as the Projects are being linked to the Results, Uses and Benefits it becomes clear that some of the proposed Results will have additional Uses. For example, schoolteachers may also shift to drinking the available and attractive water and that would lead to healthier teachers which in turn would improve the social environment for children and further motivate them to drink water.

8. Identify and where possible collect cause-and-effect Evidence that would compellingly support the linking of the potential Projects and Results to the desired Uses and Benefits:

   a. In this case, a key aspect of the Evidence will relate to whether or not the Results *really will motivate* the children to drink water. It does not matter how strongly parents, care givers and teachers believe that the children *should* drink water – what matters is whether or not the children will actually *choose* to drink water.

   b. Evidence can come from many sources such as successful similar programmes in other schools, parents' and teachers' strong commitments to the SubStrategy, changing motivations in children due to the impact of social media and so on.

   c. Such Evidence requires 4 pieces of performance management information:

      i.   The initial measurement of a causative factor;

      ii. The final measurement of a causative factor;

      iii. The initial measurement of the factor that is being influenced by the causative factor;

      iv. The final measurement of the factor that is being influenced by the causative factor.

   d. If the factor being influenced has changed following the causative factor changing then that would be, as a minimum, a correlation.

   e. If all other causes of the change to the factor being influenced have been eliminated then the four pieces of performance measurement information in 8c above amount to cause-and-effect Evidence that the causative factor is genuinely causing the changes in the factor that is being influenced.

9. Identify performance indicators which can subsequently be used to monitor and manage the Projects and to influence the Uses:

a.   Examples of performance indicators that suppliers might identify include:

     i.   the number of schools that have 'attractive' water readily available to children (this is an indicator of a Result which may or may not be Used – so while it is an easy indicator to measure to determine *progress* with the SubStrategy, it is not an indicator of *success*);

     ii.   the percentage of children who are choosing to drink water (an indicator of a Use and therefore an early *predictor* of *success*);

     iii.   the reported level of bullying of children who are overweight or trying to lose weight (an indicator of a Use, i.e. a *predictor* of *success*).

b.   As noted in Stage 1, performance indicators for Projects and Results are early measures of the *progress* of implementing a SubStrategy, *they are not measures of success!* Only indicators of Benefits (and to a lesser extent, indicators of Uses) provide convincing information about the *success* of SubStrategy implementation.

10.   Cross-check that the intended Projects and Results align with or strike a healthy balance among the agreed Values and Fundamental Principles:

a.   Suppliers of healthy water may be motivated primarily by the financial Benefits to them of securing a contract to supply water to a school, so they may not necessarily fully engage with the non-financial Values and Fundamental Principles (e.g. things like: child health; choice; learning; self-esteem; non-bullying) of this SubStrategy. This is understandable and it is not necessarily the responsibility of suppliers to directly address these Values and Fundamental Principles. However, if suppliers are not directly aligning the Projects and Results with these Values and Principles then other stakeholders need to step in and ensure this alignment.

Accountabilities in Stage 2

1.   Stage 2 *identifies* desired start-to-finish Effectiveness Accountability by identifying the *right necessary and sufficient*

Results and Projects (in that order) and checking that these Results will genuinely enable and motivate the desired Uses and Benefits.

2.   Responsibilities:

a.   In Stage 2, identifying and defining (as distinct from delivering) Effectiveness Accountability for Projects and Results and the Uses of those Results to produce Benefits is *primarily* the responsibility of purchasers.

Comments

1.   Suppliers frequently enter engagement processes with their own strong ideas on what end-users need and want. They may be correct or misguided, but either way, Stage 2 needs to start by focusing on the end-users' requirements *as identified by the end-users* i.e. their Uses and Benefits and potential Results.

2.   'Suppliers' may be in-house suppliers and not necessarily external to the organisation who is facilitating the overall strategy.

3.   It is often the case that suppliers have worked with many similar user-groups in the past, so they too will have ideas about what similar end-users want, want to do, why they want to do them and what Results will best enable those Uses. However, caution is recommended in this respect as previous situations are unlikely to be identical to the current situation.

4.   It is therefore important in Stage 2 that in addition to pursuing the requirements that end-users identified in Stage 1, that purchasers and users remain open to new ideas from suppliers, just as in Stage 1 they were open to new ideas from end-users.

5.   Any such additional Results, Uses and Benefits proposed by suppliers need to be ground-truthed with the end-user group to check that these newly proposed Results, Uses and Benefits are actually relevant for that user group.

6.   In particular, there needs to be compelling cause-and-effect Evidence that the proposed Projects will create the *right set of necessary and sufficient* Results that really will be Used to create the desired Benefits – which brings us to Stage 3 – creating

and *Validating* SubStrategies by adding convincing cause-and-effect Evidence.

So, once you have collected *actual* Uses and Benefits in Stage 1 and their enabling Results and associated Projects in Stage 2, then you are ready to move to Stage 3 – Develop Evidence-based strategies (Chapter 6).

Chapter 6
Stage 3 – Develop Evidence-based strategies

Reminder: Our purpose is *to enable and motivate Uses to create Benefits*
PRUB Mantra #1: *Only Uses create Benefits*
PRUB Mantra #2: Uses need the *right* Results or they won't happen
PRUB Mantra #3: Projects, Results, Uses and Benefits must be Linked with
compelling cause-and-effect Evidence

What is Stage 3?

Stage 3 will define and partially Validate what you intend to do (Projects), what you will produce (Results), how they will be used (Uses) and what Benefits will arise from those Uses.

Stage 3 consists of logically linking Projects and Results to Uses and Benefits and adding compelling cause-and-effect Evidence:

1. The Projects really will create the Results.
2. The Results really will enable and motivate the Uses.
3. The Uses really will create the Benefits.

What Stage 3 will achieve in order to support the other 8 stages

Stage 3 (see Figure 6.1) will create:

1. An integrated set of potential and/or existing SubStrategies, each one being logical and supported by compelling cause-and-effect Evidence.

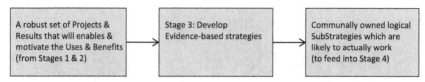

| A robust set of Projects & Results that will enables & motivate the Uses & Benefits (from Stages 1 & 2) | → | Stage 3: Develop Evidence-based strategies | → | Communally owned logical SubStrategies which are likely to actually work (to feed into Stage 4) |

Figure 6.1   The precursor to Stage 3, Stage 3 itself and what Stage 3 must feed into Stage 4.

2.   Generally, this set of SubStrategies will consist of:
      a.   a high-level Aspirational-level SubStrategy which captures on one page (15 +/– 5 PRUB boxes) the overall intentions of the strategy (See *Validating Strategies*, page 15);
      b.   a set of Guidance-level SubStrategies which provide more detail on what is intended without getting into the day-to-day operational detail (see Chapter, 10 Stage 7 "Implementation" for operational-level SubStrategies).
3.   In the case of auditing an existing strategy, Stage 3 will test the validity of the existing set of SubStrategies and indicate if the current SubStrategies are or are not:
      a.   logical;
      b.   supported by compelling Evidence that they are actually working well/optimally;
      c.   Worth It.

WHY IS STAGE 3 IMPORTANT?

1. A strategy is 'an action plan and rationale', or 'you know what you are doing and why' (Freek Vermeulen, "London Business School" in *European Business Review*, 14 January 2012). If you do not know what you are going to do and why, then, well, what are you going to do? A strategy is essential, even if it is not written down or formal in any way. The better quality the strategy, then the greater chance that desired Benefits will be achieved.

2. Through conversations with many hundreds of stakeholders, we have concluded that less than 20% and perhaps even less than 10% of existing 'strategies' make any difference. This indicates that many strategies either are not logical or are not supported by compelling Evidence that they will actually work or they are not Worth it. Applying Stage 3 to new or existing strategies is a powerful tool for determining where strategies are strong or weak in terms of their logic and/or in terms of their cause-and-effect Evidence. Stage 4 will determine whether or not they are Globally and Motivationally Worth it (see Chapter 7).

3. Frequently, there will be a number of potentially competing SubStrategies and/ or multiple strategies on related themes that need to work in parallel. Each SubStrategy needs to be *Validated* as logical and doable (this Stage 3) and Worth it (Stage 4) before decisions are made (Stage 5) on whether or not to con- tract suppliers (Stage 6) to implement (Stage 7) the preferred combination of SubStrategies.

4. A strategy is a *possible* action plan and rationale. It only gets implemented if someone *chooses* to implement it. People are more likely to choose to imple- ment a strategy if it is fully Validated and is demonstrably better than alternative strategies (or suites of SubStrategies).

5. Stage 3 is essential because it is not possible to determine if a strategy is 'Globally Worth it' (the net total Worth of the Benefits being greater than the net total costs of Projects *plus* Uses) and 'Motivationally Worth it' (each and every stakeholder gains some 'Worth' from the strategy) until the logic of the SubStrategy is confirmed and supported by compelling Evidence. Until such confirmation is in place it is impossible to correlate the Worth of the Benefits generated by a SubStrategy with those Results that are supposed to have enabled the Uses to create those Benefits. It is also impossible to cor- relate the costs of the Projects to produce those Results and the costs of the Uses required to create the Benefits. In practice, we often see unjustifiable claims made about Benefits having been created via certain Projects despite there being a lack of cause-and-effect Evidence which compellingly Links the Results through the Uses to the Benefits. SubStrategy logic and Evidence-based Validation *must* come before determining the Worth of a SubStrategy (Stage 4), hence why this Stage 3 must become *before* Stage 4.

6. In most multi-stakeholder groups, there is no shortage of good ideas about pos- sible SubStrategies which will emerge in Stages 1 and 2 of the OpenStrategies' 9-stage process. However, there is almost always a shortage of compelling Evidence that:

    a. the Projects *logically* Link via Results and Uses to Benefits;

    b. the Projects will *actually* create the desired Results and that the Results will *actually* be Used and that the Uses will *actually* generate the desired Benefits;

    c. the SubStrategies are both 'Globally and Motivationally Worth it' (see Stage 4, Chapter 7);

    d. the proposed SubStrategies are the *best* SubStrategies or the *best combina- tion* of SubStrategies (Stage 5, Chapter 8).

7. So, a strategy and its component SubStrategies, need to be *Validated* (*Validating Strategies*, page 210).

Summary of the start-to-finish action sequence for Stage 3

1. **DRIC.** Use DRIC to refine the *logic* of the rough SubStrategies arising from Stage 2. DRIC = **D**istil; **R**efine; **I**nfer; **C**reate (see *Validating Strategies*, page 162).
    a. **Distil.** Review the rough SubStrategies from Stages 1 and 2 and distil those Projects, Results, Uses and Benefits which meet the Values and Fundamental Principles that the stakeholders have defined in Stages 1 and 2.
    b. **Refine.** Reword the Projects, Results, Uses and Benefits so that they are succinct and crystal clear and can be understood by all stakeholders.
    c. **Infer.** Infer missing Projects, Results, Uses and Benefits where it is straightforward to do so.
    d. **Create.** Create new Projects, Results, Uses and Benefits to fill any remaining gaps in the SubStrategy.
2. **Validate.** Add cause-and-effect Evidence to every Link to confirm that the SubStrategies *really will work*.
3. **Performance indicators:** Fine-tune the performance indicators associated with each Project, Result, Use and Benefit so that *progress* (lead indicators) and *success* (lag indicators) are clearly defined.

Explanation of the start-to-finish action sequence for Stage 3

1. **DRIC.** Use DRIC to refine the *logic* of the rough SubStrategies arising from Stage 2.
    a. **Distil.** Review the rough SubStrategies from Stages 1 and 2 (for new or for existing strategies) and Distil those Projects, Results, Uses and Benefits which meet the Values and Fundamental Principles criteria that the stakeholders have defined in Stages 1 and 2. If relevant, eliminate some of the potential Uses and Benefits that are outside the scope of the purchaser's remit or transfer them to other organisations. Usually

this can be done by the group facilitator without too much reference back to the stakeholders. However, creating these draft SubStrategies needs to be done with great care because although the Uses and Benefits might be outside the remit of the purchaser, they may nevertheless:

i.   be very important to end-users, since if the Uses and Benefits are summarily discarded by purchasers without convincing justification, end-users will lose faith in the purchasers;

ii.   be within the remit of the end-users and/or of other potential suppliers;

iii.   be creatively enabled by the Projects and Results that are going to happen anyway;

iv.   be creatively enabled by Projects and Results that suppliers are prepared to run in parallel with those Projects and Results purchased by the purchaser.

b.   **Refine**. Precisely reword the Projects, Results, Uses and Benefits so that they are succinct and crystal clear and can be understood by all stakeholders as well as being logically linked to all other PRUBs. This is a challenging step but one which is essential for meaningful and unequivocal communications amongst stakeholders. To become proficient in this task typically takes several days training and practice in PRUB-Logic. This is because although PRUB-Logic seems obvious and simple, the world is complex. This in turn means that it is challenging to translate the complexity of the world into simple, PRUB-based strategies. Usually this 'refine' task can be done by a group facilitator with minimal reference back to stakeholders. The next section in this chapter provides some examples of how end-user statements can be refined into more meaningfully worded Projects, Results, Uses and Benefits.

c.   **Infer**. Usually there will be gaps in the rough SubStrategies from Stage 2, for example, where a Project has been defined but its Results were deemed so obvious that they were not written down. It is important to fill in these gaps because what might be 'obvious' to one stakeholder is very often not obvious to others (or other stakeholders may reach an equally obvious but divergent conclusion). In this 'infer' step, it is important to infer only those concepts which are unequivocally true. Usually 'infer' can be done by a group facilitator although it will generally pay to share the inferences with a cross-section of stakeholders to check that they are accurate and relevant. See the example that follows on the hypothetical but realistic Pingo water quality strategy.

d.   **Create**. After the 'infer' step, there will usually still be gaps in the SubStrategies. At this point it is appropriate to 'create' new Projects, Results, Uses and Benefits to fill the remaining gaps. It is strongly recommended that this step be undertaken through engagement with at least a representative cross-section of stakeholders and that most stakeholders then be consulted on any newly created SubStrategies.

The steps of 'infer' and 'create' necessarily overlap depending on the skill and sector-knowledge of the facilitator. For example, if there is a Use of 'people are catching fish in the river' then anyone could infer a Result that 'there are fish in the river'. However, if a Result is 'rivers are free of nutrient run-off', a skilled and informed facilitator would probably infer that 'farmers have installed riparian plantings and fencing to keep stock out of rivers' whereas someone less knowledgeable about land and water management would need to 'create', rather than 'infer', these concepts of riparian planting and fencing

Either way, 'infer' and 'create' are about filling in the gaps in the information that stakeholders have generated

A key factor here is to build confidence that the proposed Results are not only *necessary* (i.e. you have compelling cause-and-effect Evidence that they will definitely be Used) but also that they are *sufficient* to *enable and motivate Uses to create Benefits*. Over and over again we have seen excellent Results that are not being Used because on their own they were *necessary but not sufficient* to enable the Uses, maybe because no-one knew about them or because they were not readily accessible. So, it is not sufficient to simply have good Results. People need to know about them, the Results need to be accessible and end-users need to be sufficiently motivated and skilled to Use them

This is a particularly good time in the process to check back with end-users to refresh your understanding of exactly what they want to do (Uses) and why (Benefits) and to ask *them* if the proposed set of Results is indeed necessary and sufficient

2.   **Validate**. Add cause-and-effect Evidence to confirm that the SubStrategies *really will work*. Cause-and-effect Evidence sits on the Links between:

   I.   Projects and Results (Evidence that a Project really will produce the Result);

   II.   Results and Uses (Evidence that a Result really will be Used);

   III.   Uses and Benefits (Evidence that a Use really will create the intended Benefits).

   a.   This step is one of the most difficult because genuine cause-and-effect Evidence is hard to find. Cause-and-effect Evidence is not just 'correlation' or 'information' and it is certainly not just 'data'. 'X happens and then Y happens immediately after' indicates a correlation between X and Y but that does not mean that X caused Y (see *Validating Strategies*, pages 34, 35).

   b.   So, for example, '1000 children per day are swimming in the swimming pool' is a single piece of data. It is not cause-and-effect Evidence.

   c.   In contrast, information such as: "the price of entry to the swimming pool was lowered by 50% and the number of children swimming in the swimming pool increased from 1000/day to 1,500/day" is definitely a correlation. It may also be cause-and-effect Evidence if nothing else changed at the same time. For example, the higher fee might have been charged in winter and the lower fee in summer, so the increase in numbers of children swimming in the swimming pool might have been due to the change of season, not due to the change in the entry fee.

   d.   But let's say that nothing else changed and that the change in the fee was in fact the cause of the increase in the number of children using the pool. Note that this cause-and-effect Evidence requires *four pieces of data*:

i.   the initial fee;
ii.   the subsequent fee;
iii.   the initial number of children swimming in the swimming pool;
iv.   the subsequent number of children swimming in the swimming pool.

So, each piece of cause-and-effect Evidence requires *four pieces of data*: the original and final states of factor 'A' that is doing the causing and the initial and final states of factor 'B' that is experiencing the effects. It is frequently challenging to find such information as a correlation, let alone as cause-and-effect Evidence. However, it is highly risky to implement strategies if they are not supported by compelling cause-and-effect Evidence on every single link.

e.   It is usually safe to rely on suppliers to provide cause-and-effect Evidence that Projects will produce the desired Results, especially if the suppliers are accredited to ISO 9003 or better. Suppliers can generally exert a high degree of 'control' over their Projects to make sure that they produce the desired Results.

f.   Cause-and-effect Evidence that Uses will produce the desired Benefits is frequently possible to find in the form of examples of similar Uses elsewhere in the world which confirm whether or not those Uses did in fact generate the desired Results.

g.   However, when it comes to finding cause-and-effect Evidence that your particular cohort of users will definitely Use your proposed set of Results, it becomes much more problematic. In our experience, this is the most important set of cause-and-effect Evidence because so many strategies fail because Results are not Used as predicted.

h.   Uses are almost always voluntary, so Uses cannot be *controlled*: they can only be *influenced* by providing the *right* Results, which are both *necessary and sufficient*, that are readily *accessible* and which users *know about* are *capable* of Using and are *motivated* to Use. So, pieces of cause-and-effect Evidence are required for each of these factors in order to build up confidence that Results really will be Used as intended.

i. It is essential to distinguish between what end-users *say* they will do and what they will *actually* do if certain Results are made available. Many people *say* they want to go to the gym and exercise to get fit when in reality they may go once or twice and then find excuses not to go (indeed the profitability of many commercial gyms relies on paid-up members not using the gym).

j. It is seldom possible to find 100% convincing cause-and-effect Evidence that Results really will be Used as predicted. Stakeholders therefore usually need to make partially informed judgements about whether or not to proceed with a SubStrategy based on incomplete Evidence.

k. In such circumstances, stakeholders (particularly pur-chasers) may commission various forms of market research (questionnaires; focus groups; Agile-style rapid and repeated prototyping-and-end-user-testing; workshops; test marketing and so on) to generate more convincing Evidence. In all cases, the *purpose* of these methods is to better understand Uses, Benefits and their enabling and motivating Results so as to find cause-and-effect Evidence that is so compelling that it justifies making the necessary investments in Projects to generate the required Results. And in all cases, these market-research methods need to ask end-users what they want to *do* (Uses) and *why* (Benefits) and then, and only then, what necessary and sufficient set of Results do users *want* (See *Validating Strategies*, page 87).

l. Because end-users cannot be *controlled* (Uses are vol-untary), it is challenging to fully understand and find compelling cause-and-effect Evidence for Uses, moti-vations for Uses to create Benefits and the necessary and sufficient set of Results to enable and motivate those Uses.

m. However, if you do not have compelling cause-and-effect Evidence to *Validate* your strategies, then you *cannot have confidence in making and implementing deci-sions about which SubStrategies are Worth investing in.* So, it is essential that the Projects, Results, Uses and Benefits that have emerged in Stages 1 and 2 be translated into compellingly Evidenced SubStrategies before attempt-ing to determine the *Global and Motivational Worth* of the SubStrategies (Stage 4) or make investment deci-sions about them (Stage 5).

3.   **Performance indicators.** Fine-tune the performance indica-tors associated with each Project, Result, Use and Benefit so that *progress* (lead indicators) and *success* (lag indicators) are clearly defined:

   a.   Stage 3 is where it is time to get serious about identify-ing and selecting the *right* performance indicators.

   b.   Indicators need to **indicate** *something that you can act on and manage.* Indicators are not just random things that can be measured; that's data. Indicators need to tell you if your strategy implementation is on track and if not then they need to *indicate* where and how you might get the strategy back on track. More than one indicator may need to be monitored and managed in order to successfully keep strategy implementation on track.

   c.   So, the need for an indicator to *indicate something useful* parallels Cochrane's aphorism (slightly edited to suit this context):

   > "Before measuring something, decide what you will do if the answer is too high, just right or too low. If what you will do in each situation is the same then do not make the measurement" (the original aphorism is: "Before ordering a test, decide what you will do if it is (1) positive or (2) negative. If both answers are the same, do not take the test". http://community-archive.cochrane.org/about-us/history/archie-cochrane)

   d.   Is a measure of Project expenditure a useful 'indica-tor'? Not necessarily. Expenditure may be running ahead of schedule but that may be because the Project is also running ahead of schedule. So while it is easy to measure expenditure it is seldom *sufficient* information for guiding improved management of Projects.

e. So, in Stage 3, review the performance indicators that end-users, suppliers and others have proposed and check that they:

   i. really are *indicators* that you can *act* on;
   ii. are a *sufficient* set of indicators to guide strategic actions (you will probably need to identify additional ones and eliminate some that add minimal worth for subsequent performance management);
   iii. are able to be effectively and efficiently measured and understood;
   iv. include both lead indicators (relating to Projects and Results) for monitoring and *managing progress* with strategy implementation and lag indicators (relating to Uses and Benefits) for monitoring and *influencing success*;

f. performance indicators relating to:

   i. Projects will measure progress with suppliers' actions;
   ii. Results will measure the quality and quantity of the things that suppliers have created;
   iii. Uses will measure progress with end-users' actions;
   iv. Benefits will measure success with Benefits.

Demonstration of Stage 3 actions

As with the strategy on the rejuvenation of a CBD and the obesity strategy (see Stages 1 and 2 above), the environment is complex so the following hypothetical example SubStrategy on the management of water quality in the Pingo River is necessarily incomplete. However, it serves the purpose of demonstrating how an understanding of Uses by different entities (people, fish, birds, plants) guides what is needed in terms of Projects and Results. Once these ideals have been identified they can then be fleshed out in more detail, business cases developed and prioritised and preferred SubStrategies selected, contracted-for, implemented and performance-managed to optimise Benefits.

1. **DRIC**. Use DRIC to refine the *logic* of the rough SubStrategies arising from Stage 2 (**D**istil; **R**efine; **I**nfer; **C**reate (*Validating Strategies*, page 162).

    a. **Distil**. Review the rough SubStrategies from Stages 1 and 2 and distil those Projects, Results, Uses and Benefits which meet the Values and Fundamental Principles criteria for the purchaser and its stakeholders:

        i.   Table 6.1 shows some of the raw data that was generated by end-users, suppliers and other stakeholders for the hypothetical environmental strategy on the Pingo River.

        ii. The statements in Table 6.1 are not precisely worded Projects or Results or Uses or Benefits. Nevertheless, they contain good information that can be readily distilled into an early-draft SubStrategy such as shown in Figure 6.2.

        iii. The words from the table have been distilled directly into the draft SubStrategy – they have not been edited in this first task (**D**istil) of Stage 3. It is important to *not* edit them until they are embedded in the draft SubStrategy because the SubStrategy starts to show their relationships with other pieces of information and that guides the next task: refining the wordings.

Table 6.1   **This table contains the types of statements that typically emerge from conversations with end-users and suppliers. They are not succinctly worded as Projects, Results, Uses and Benefits but they are good start**

- We want to safely eat fish and watercress from the Pingo River.
- We need the right amount of watercress in the river because too much will block the flow.
- We do not want to get sick from eating the fish and watercress from the Pingo River.
- We want fish and birds to be thriving in the Pingo River.
- We think it would be good if children could find out more about the ecology of the Pingo River.
- Can landholders do something about pollution entering the river?
- How good does water quality have to be so that the fish and watercress are safe to eat?

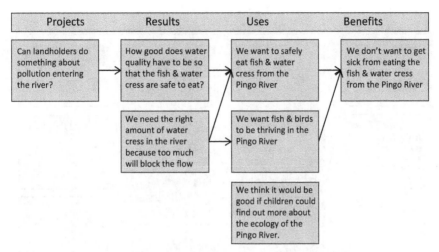

Projects	Results	Uses	Benefits
Can landholders do something about pollution entering the river?	How good does water quality have to be so that the fish & water cress are safe to eat?	We want to safely eat fish & water cress from the Pingo River	We don't want to get sick from eating the fish & water cress from the Pingo River
	We need the right amount of water cress in the river because too much will block the flow	We want fish & birds to be thriving in the Pingo River	
		We think it would be good if children could find out more about the ecology of the Pingo River.	

Figure 6.2   A *loosely worded* SubStrategy on the Pingo River *Distilled* (but not yet refined) from stakeholder inputs.

b.   **Refine.** Reword the Projects, Results, Uses and Benefits so that they are succinct and crystal clear and can be understood by all stakeholders:

i.   Refining the wording in Figure 6.2 would lead to Figure 6.3

ii.   here are some of the reasons for the rewordings:

1.   Written stakeholder submissions will capture only some of the communications (workshops, emails, phone calls) that will take place during the development of a strategy. The non-written concepts can be added by the facilitator during this strategy refinement Stage 3 subject to then checking their accuracy with key stakeholders.

2.   Result #1 was reworded from being a question to being a statement about the quality of the water, albeit without any clarity (yet) on what is meant by 'good' water quality. The question has been left in the Result box so that in a later part of Stage 3 it can be addressed (see 'Performance Indicators' below).

3.   Use #2 was reworded as an actual Use, i.e. an *action* that people actually want to do (eat fish and watercress) rather than on them 'wanting' to do something. Uses are best worded by starting the sentence by describing the *end*-Use (eating fish

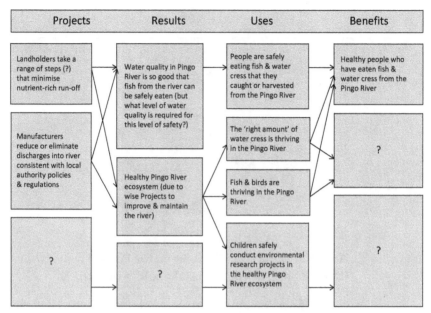

Projects	Results	Uses	Benefits

Figure 6.3   The Pingo River Aspirational-level SubStrategy as Distilled *and Refined* from the raw material collected from stakeholders. The refinement is based on stakeholders' written statements (see Table 6.1) *plus the facilitator's own records of other statements made in stakeholder workshops.*

and watercress), then followed in the sentence by earlier actions (catch fish and harvest watercress in the Pingo River). So, the Use was refined to: "People are safely eating fish & watercress that they caught or harvested from the Pingo River".

4.   So, a Use focuses on the user *doing something* and not on the user *using something*. This difference is subtle but important. Certainly a Use involves using a Result but in this instance, a person is not going to think to themselves: "I'll go and *Use* the river to catch fish in"; they will think "I'll go and catch fish (in the river)". 'Catching fish' is a much clearer and more intended Use than 'Using the river'. It also focuses the mind on the user doing something that is important to them ('market-pull'), rather than on trying to find a Use for a Result ('product-push').

5.   Use #3 has been reworded to focus on what children will actually be doing (if the SubStrategy

can subsequently be *Validated)* and not on what other stakeholders think they *ought* to be doing. It also makes a clearer statement about the specific actions the children will be doing ('safely conducting environmental research Projects') and the conditions under which they will do this ('in the healthy Pingo River ecosystem').

c.   **Infer**. Infer missing Projects, Results, Uses and Benefits where it is straightforward to do so: In this example, an informed facilitator could *reasonably infer* the following additional hypothetical Projects and Benefits:

    i.   Inferred reworded Project: "Landholders fence off rivers and streams and do riparian planting which minimises nutrient-rich run-off". It could be argued that this riparian planting is a 'created' concept (see step 'd'). However, in the area of land and water management, riparian planting and fencing are some of the most common forms of protecting waterways, so it would be reasonable to 'infer' these actions. In a different context (e.g. stock management), 'riparian planting' could not so easily be inferred and might appear under 'd' as a created new concept.

    ii.   Inferred Project: 'Schools develop environmental courses for children based on the Pingo River ecosystem'.

    iii.   Inferred Benefit: 'Children have a deep appreciation of the Worths of healthy river ecosystems'.

d.   **Create**. Create new Projects, Results, Uses and Benefits to fill any remaining gaps in the SubStrategy. In this example, it might be reasonable for a skilled facilitator to help stakeholders to *create* the following hypothetical Projects, Results, Uses and Benefits:

    i.   New Use = "Tourists pay for and use boat trips on the river";

    ii.   New Benefit = "Sustainable businesses for boat trip operators";

    iii.   New Result = "Piers for boat trip business";

    iv.   New Project = "Build piers and supporting infrastructure for boat trip operators";

  v. New Use = "Tourists pay for and take part in environmental courses originally designed for children";

  vi. New Benefit = "Environmental courses are more sustainable due to income from tourists".

The more complete Aspirational-level SubStrategy is shown in Figure 6.4.

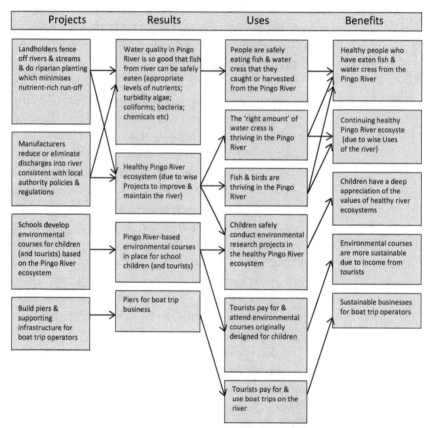

Figure 6.4 **The evolving Aspirational-level SubStrategy on environmentally sound Uses of the Pingo River.**

  Because of the complexity of this and many other strategies, a series of interlinked *sub*-SubStrategies would be required to fully address water quality in the Pingo River. For example, at least four *sub*-SubStrategies would be required addressing, respectively, each of the four Projects:

  1. Landholders fence off rivers and streams and do riparian planting which minimises nutrient-rich run-off.

2.   Manufacturers reduce or eliminate discharges into the river consistent with local authority policies and regulations, also leading to cleaner rivers and manufacturers retaining their social licence to operate as they are seen to be looking after the environment.

3.   Schools develop environmental courses for children (and tourists) based on the Pingo River ecosystem.

4.   Build piers in the Pingo River for use by commercial boat operators.

It is also possible that the second SubStrategy above ("Manufacturers …") would need to be broken down into several even more detailed *sub*-Sub-Strategies, one for each category of manufacturer.

Every SubStrategy and every level of Sub-SubStrategy Uses the same PRUB-format and is limited to 15 +/–5 boxes of information. This consistency and suc-cinctness of language greatly help all stakeholders to understand each SubStrategy and each level of SubStrategy.

In the real world, this Pingo River SubStrategy would involve many stakeholders including local authorities, indigenous groups, the Ministries of Health and Agriculture, environmental groups (represent-ing themselves and the environment itself), recreational groups, foresters, schoolteachers, landholders, Four Wheel Drive (4WD) clubs, water scien-tists, construction companies and others.

The DRIC process demonstrates that it is straightforward to use PRUB-Logic to convert a fairly rough set of stakeholders' ideas into a rea-sonable-looking SubStrategy that makes sense. Note, however, that this SubStrategy already contains 19 boxes of information. A SubStrategy of this size will already be stretching the cognitive limits of some stakehold-ers so it must not get any bigger.

If additional ideas need to be added, then some of the existing ideas will need to be condensed into fewer boxes e.g. the two Uses of: "children … and tourists … carrying out environmental research projects" could be amalgamated.

If at the same time, more detail is required, then while leaving the Aspirational SubStrategy unchanged it would be appropriate to cre-ate sub-SubStrategies on those topics that need more detail. For exam-ple, the first Project "Landholders fence off rivers and streams and do riparian planting which minimises nutrient-rich run-off" might be expanded into a subSubStrategy along the following lines (see Figure 6.5).

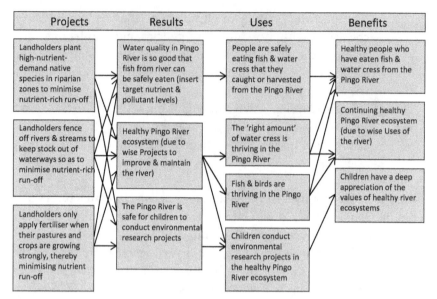

Figure 6.5   A *sub*-SubStrategy focusing on better management of nutrient run-off into the Pingo River ecosystem.

Landholders are likely to relate to this more detailed *sub*-SubStrategy because it provides more guidance than the Aspirational SubStrategy. In practice, they may need even more details added to create an Operational-level SubStrategy. They will particularly want to know "what Benefits will landholders receive to motivate them to act?" As currently worded the SubStrategy doesn't offer much incentive for farmers so it would not be surprising if they lacked enthusiasm for spending money on fencing and riparian planting.

Many of the other stakeholders will probably be perfectly happy with the level of detail in the Aspirational SubStrategy and/or they may wish to create their own more detailed sub-SubStrategies, for example, on the details of developing the environmental education courses; building the piers and running a sustainable boating business; and so on. This confirms that different stakeholders want different levels of detail in their strategies but at the same time they also want to understand the higher-level strategies that are 'above' their own strategies and the lower level strategies that are 'below' their own strategies.

In each case, the same PRUB-Logic-based strategy format enables all the SubStrategies to be readily compared; interlinked and understood.

Only one strategy-structure needs to be understood – and it is the simple PRUB-Logic structure: "the smallest amount of strategic information that has the highest value to the most stakeholders".

2.   **Validate**. Add cause-and-effect Evidence to confirm that the SubStrategies *really will work*. Here are some examples of possible cause-and-effect Evidence for this hypothetical but realistic SubStrategy. These examples demonstrate that there are different categories of Evidence including, but not limited to, historical Evidence, Evidence-from-elsewhere, scientific Evidence, and end-user-statement Evidence.

    a.   *Historical Validation: What is the Evidence for the Links from Result #1 to Use #1 and to Benefit #1?* Historically people have safely eaten fish and watercress in the Pingo River but it has not been safe to do so in the last 10 years. As the pollution is cleaned up there is a high degree of confidence that food from the river will again be safe to eat and people will again harvest and eat it and be healthy.

    b.   *Evidence-from-elsewhere   Validation   (precedents-based Validation): What is the Evidence for the Links from Project #3 to Result #3, Use #4 and Benefit #3?* Similar courses are successfully run in three other cities in the country and they have been well patronised by older children in the local schools' environmental programmes so there is a high degree of confidence that such courses will be well patronised in the Pingo River ecosystem.

    c.   *Scientific Validation: What is the Evidence for the Links from Projects 1 and 2 to Results 1 and 2?* There is robust scientific Evidence such as ecological modelling shows that within 5 years the proposed Projects will bring the Pingo River water quality up to the standards required for fish and their food sources to thrive.

    d.   *End-user statements Validation: What is the Evidence that Use 1 will happen and will result in Benefit 1?* End-users state confidently that they will harvest and eat fish and watercress from the Pingo River once the river water quality is of high enough standard. End-users state confidently that they feel healthier when they can consume food from healthy rivers. Such end-user statements are often not as reliable as historical or scientific or precedent-based Evidence but in many instances they may be the only Evidence available. Such Evidence will carry the most weight if it has been distilled using suitably worded questions within representative market research in a large sample.

3. **Performance indicators:** fine-tune the performance indicators associated with each Project, Result, Use and Benefit so that *progress* (lead indicators) and *success* (lag indicators) are clearly defined:

    a. For Result #1 in Figure 6.5: indicators might include: nitrate levels; phosphate levels; faecal coliform levels (all indicative of nutrient run-off); heavy metals levels; solvent levels (both indicative of industrial pollution). These are lead indicators. The target levels of these indicators also need to be determined, either in this Stage or by Stage 6 (contracts).

    b. For Result #3 in Figure 6.4: an indicator might be: the quality, availability and accessibility of online and in-stream research-learning modules for children's environmental courses. This is a lead indicator.

    c. For Use #4 in Figure 6.4: the number of schools that are sending classes of older children to the environmental research programme based on the Pingo River ecosystem. This is a lag indicator.

    d. For Project #2 in Figure 6.4: the percentage of manufacturers who are running clean-up programmes which will reduce discharges to acceptable levels within 12 months. This is a lead indicator.

    e. For Benefit #3 in Figure 6.4: the number of children who are enthusiastic about using their local stretch of the Pingo River for recreation *after* their research project and/or their level of enthusiasm for taking part in future river restoration Projects alongside landholders. These are lag indicators.

Accountabilities in Stage 3

1. Identifying and defining Benefits-Effectiveness (compellingly determining that Worthwhile Benefits will definitely arise from the Uses) is *primarily* the responsibility of purchasers but unequivocally needs input from suppliers and end-users.

2. Identifying and defining Projects-Efficiency (compellingly determining that the Projects will definitely create the Results) is *primarily* the responsibility of the suppliers.

3. Identifying and defining Uses-Efficiency (compellingly determining that the Results will definitely be Efficiently Used) is *primarily* the responsibility of purchasers and is the most difficult Efficiency Accountability to identify, quantify and implement.

Comments

1. Of overwhelming importance is the cause-and-effect Evidence that Results really will be Used. In our experience this is the exact point where many strategies fail. As discussed in detail in *Validating Strategies*, Chapters 1 and 2, there is a 'handover' of ownership of actions and consequences between different stakeholders from Results (created by suppliers) to Uses (by end-users). This handover cannot be compelled or managed or required or in any other way enforced. Even in a school setting children cannot be forced to engage in environmental programmes. Certainly, reasonably strong pressures can be applied to encourage children to participate but such pressure will not be nearly as effective as making the programmes so attractive that the children are *motivated* to participate. So, almost without exception, Uses are voluntary, so the Results must be compellingly attractive and the Uses must be motivated by Worthwhile Benefits, otherwise Uses of Results simply will not happen.

2. SubStrategies based on PRUB-Logic provide a succinct and clear structure for defining *exactly* which information is required to create a compellingly Evidenced SubStrategy. ("*The smallest amount of strategic information that has the highest*

value to the most stakeholders"). In addition to the PRUB-Logic sequences which form the basis of a SubStrategy, cause-and-effect Evidence is required. This Evidence is required precisely on the Links between Projects, Results, Uses and Benefits, so PRUB-Logic provides excellent guidance on where to look for the most relevant Evidence.

3.   Crucially, the development/refinement of a strategy should not be confused with decisions on whether or not to implement a strategy. A Validated strategy or set of SubStrategies defines what *can* genuinely happen and what *will* be Worth doing but decisions on whether or not to allocate resources to such strategies are *outside the strategy*. This is important because if resource limitations are introduced too soon into a strategy development/review process they can seriously limit thinking.

4.   So, it is essential to create and review strategies *without assuming limited resources* because once strategies and their Benefits to multiple stakeholders are clear, unexpected resources can often turn up to enable the strategies to be implemented.

So, once you have logical SubStrategies that are supported by compelling cause-and-effect Evidence that confirms that they definitely can work, then you are ready to move to Stage 4 – determining if a SubStrategy is *Worth it* (Chapter 7).

Chapter 7

Stage 4 – Validate strategies by determining their Worth

Reminder: Our purpose is *to enable and motivate Uses to create Benefits*

PRUB Mantra #1: *Only Uses create Benefits*

PRUB Mantra #2: Uses need the *right* Results or they won't happen

PRUB Mantra #3: Projects, Results, Uses and Benefits must be Linked with compelling Evidence

PRUB Mantra #4: SubStrategies must be both Globally and Motivationally Worth it

What is Stage 4?

Stage 4 will enable stakeholders to objectively articulate, contrast and compare the costs and Benefits of various SubStrategies to decide if they are 'Worth it' and so guide subsequent investment decisions.

Stage 4 consists of:

1. Confirming that the consolidated Worth of all the Benefits in each SubStrategy or business case is greater than the costs of all the Projects *plus* the costs of all the Uses in each SubStrategy ('Global Worth').

2. Confirming that each and every stakeholder obtains sufficient Worth to motivate them to make their necessary contributions to implementing the strategy ('Motivational Worth').

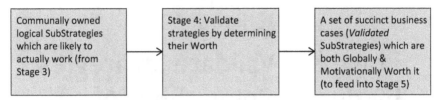

| Communally owned logical SubStrategies which are likely to actually work (from Stage 3) | → | Stage 4: Validate strategies by determining their Worth | → | A set of succinct business cases (*Validated* SubStrategies) which are both Globally & Motivationally Worth it (to feed into Stage 5) |

Figure 7.1   **The precursor to Stage 4, Stage 4 itself and what Stage 4 must feed into Stage 5.**

What Stage 4 will achieve in order to support the other 8 stages

Stage 4 will generate:

1.   A complementary and/or competing suite of potential, *Validated* SubStrategies, each one compellingly demonstrating that the total consolidated *Worth* of all the Benefits is greater than the costs of all the Projects *plus* the cost of all the Uses (Global Worth).

2.   The suite of *Validated* SubStrategies must *also* demonstrate that every stakeholder (especially end-users) who is required to contribute to the success of the SubStrategy will gain suffi-cient *Worth* to motivate their contributions. This means that the Worth of the Benefits *to each key stakeholder* must be greater than the costs *to them* of the Projects *plus* the costs *to them* of the Uses (Motivational Worth) (see Figure 7.1)

WHY IS STAGE 4 IMPORTANT?

1. 'Worth' can be economic, social, environmental or cultural.
2. Similarly, costs can be economic, social, environmental or cultural.
3. In most multi-stakeholder groups, there is no shortage of good ideas about what Projects could be run. In contrast, there is almost always a dearth of compelling Evidence that the combined Worth of all the Benefits (Global Worth) is greater than the *combined* cost of Projects *plus* Uses.

4. There is also seldom objective information that the Worth to each and every stakeholder (Motivational Worth) is sufficient to motivate them to make their necessary contributions to implementing the strategy. This is particularly the case when a Use generates a Benefit for someone other than the user. For example, the wise Use of land by a farmer will generate a primary Benefit of a healthy environment which benefits the environment itself and the many other users of that environment. The landowner will also Benefit from a clean environment but the Worth of that Benefit may not be enough to motivate them. In this case in may be necessary to identify additional Benefits that will in fact motivate the land owner. For example, a Benefit of 'farmers have a social licence to operate due to their wise Use of their land' may have sufficient Motivational Worth that the farmers feel inspired to incur the costs of managing their land wisely (including *Projects* that improve the land as an asset as well as *Uses* that Use that asset to create Benefits – including a long-term healthy ecosystem). Alternatively, it may be possible to reduce the costs to farmers of the Projects so that their Benefits/Costs ratio improves enough to motivate them.

5. Almost always there will not be enough resources to implement all potential SubStrategies, so it is necessary to select only the best ones. The best ones will be those that are *Validated* (logical; will definitely work; and Globally and Motivationally Worth it) as well as being the *most* Worth-it (better than competing SubStrategies) and also meeting other stakeholder criteria (affordability; social and political acceptability and so on) as determined in Stage 1.

6. SubStrategies must be both 'Globally Worth it' and Motivationally Worth it. So for example, while reduced obesity and diabetes due to overweight people living healthier lives will create huge savings in the health system, such savings may not compellingly motivate overweight people to change their lifestyles because such changes are often incredibly difficult to make. So to be successful, a SubStrategy to reduce obesity and diabetes must be sufficiently enabling and must generate sufficiently Worthwhile Benefits for overweight people such that they are sufficiently *motivated and able* to change their lifestyles.

7. So, before decisions can be made to implement one or more SubStrategies it is necessary to know if they are *both* Globally and Motivationally Worth it. Stage 3 provided compelling Evidence that the proposed Projects and Results would indeed enable and would theoretically motivate the desired Benefits. However, Stage 3 didn't determine the Worth of those Benefits and therefore didn't quantify if the *sizes and distribution* of the Global and Motivational Worths are sufficient to motivate the stakeholders to make the strategy succeed, hence why Stage 4 is important.

8. *The linking of Projects via Results and Uses to Benefits had to be done* **before** *it was possible to determine the Global or Motivational Worth of a SubStrategy because the Worth calculation needed to know for certain which Projects would genuinely enable and motivate which Benefits. Until such linking is confirmed, it is simply not possible to objectively correlate Benefits with Projects to determine Global and Motivational Worths.*

9. So, PRUB-Logic helps define the Benefits and who gains them. Asking users about the Worth, to them, of the Benefits goes a long way towards determining the Global and Motivational Worths of each SubStrategy. However, for very large scale initiatives it is likely that it will require professional analysts (e.g. in government departments or Treasury) to calculate the full economic, social, cultural and environmental Worths of all the Benefits. The key point is that in making these calculations, these professionals will be able to work with clearly articulated Benefits *as determined by those who are gaining the Benefits* and not some idealised Benefits determined by other stakeholders (e.g. suppliers who are trying to justify their Projects).

10. 'Worth' means different things to different people and can be economic, social, environmental or cultural (the 'four well-beings'). End-users' Benefits and Worths can be difficult for suppliers and purchasers to determine, so it is imperative to determine end-users' Benefits and Worths by asking end-users to identify *their* Benefits and to put *their* Worths on the Benefits. This is especially the case with Benefits to end-users who are seldom motivated by global Benefits (such as saving money in the health system) and are usually more motivated by Benefits with high Motivational Worth, i.e. which are personal to them.

11. It is essential that such Worths be identified and quantified for each and every type of Worth so that the Global and Motivational Worths of a SubStrategy can be determined ready for comparing with the Global and Motivational Worths of other, potentially competing SubStrategies in Stage 5.

12. When making investment decisions (Stage 5), fully *Validated* SubStrategies are easy to compare with each other because they use the same simple language and logical and financial constructs for determining Global and Motivational Worths.

13. In order to limit the time/resources spent on conducting full Better Business Case or Investment Logic Mapping investigations for a large spectrum of SubStrategies, *Validated*, SubStrategies are excellent for triaging and short listing preferred SubStrategies for subsequent BBC/ILM analysis.

Summary of the start-to-finish action sequence for Stage 4

1.   Identify, quantify and add up the costs of all the Projects.
2.   Identify, quantify and add up the true costs to each user of each Use and multiply by the number of Uses and frequency and duration of Uses.
3.   Determine the Global and Motivational Worths of the Benefits and hence the 'Worth' of the SubStrategy both globally and to each stakeholder.
4.   If necessary, upgrade the SubStrategy so that:
      a.   it will produce sufficient Global Worth;
      b.   it will produce sufficient Motivational Worth for each and every key stakeholder.
5.   If sufficiently compelling Motivational Worth cannot be created then, *as a last resort*, consider if some form of regulation or coercion can be applied to 'encourage' those stakeholders to contribute as required for implementing the SubStrategy.
6.   Confirm the most relevant performance indicators and targets associated with each Project, Result, Use and Benefit.

Explanation of the start-to-finish action sequence for Stage 4

1.   Identify, quantify and add up the costs of each Project.
      a.   Financial costs can generally be easily determined.
      b.   Social, environmental and cultural costs are generally more difficult to determine but they can be very significant. For example, the export of pure mountain water by installing dams and pipelines from the Alps to a coastal loading wharf for tankers would have:
            i.   many environmental costs including the impact on landscapes, flora and fauna of the dams, pipelines and loading wharfs; the risk of tankers discharging contaminated foreign water into a pure environment;

ii.   numerous cultural costs for the many people who value pure water as sacrosanct and which should never be treated as a commodity for commercial gain;

iii. many social costs in terms of the negative impacts for many people on their enjoyment of the natural environment.

There are many methodologies for determining the non-financial costs/values such as (examples only):

https://ssir.org/articles/entry/measuring_social_value

https://www.landcareresearch.co.nz/__data/assets/pdf_file/0019/77050/2_4_Clough.pdf

https://www.investopedia.com/terms/i/imputed-value.asp

Therefore, these and related methods will not be discussed here. The key point is that PRUB-Logic identifies precisely where these costs arise (within Projects *and* Uses) so they can be included in the calculations of Worths.

2.   Identify, quantify and add up the true costs to each user of each Use and multiply by the number of Uses and frequency and duration of Uses. Use costs may include:

a.   the cost of travel to the location where a Result is available plus admission and parking fees (e.g. a hospital, library, healthy river ecosystem, CBD);

b.   the costs of accommodation at that location (e.g. caregivers staying in hotels near a regional hospital where their loved one is being treated, invariably being more expensive than staying in their own homes while their loved ones are treated in local community hospitals);

c.   the costs of finding out about a Result;

d.   the costs of learning how to Use a Result;

e.   the capital and ongoing costs of users purchasing their own resources in order to Use a Result (e.g. purchasing a bicycle in order to use a cycleway as well as an employer providing bike parking and showers for cyclists who have cycled to work);

f.   the mental and emotional costs to a patient who is submitting themselves to surgery (which is a Use in which the patient, not the surgeon, is the primary actor/user);

g.   the costs to other stakeholders due to a Use (e.g. the mental and emotional costs of additional traffic noise for residents living near a new motorway).

3.   Determine the Global and Motivational Worth of the Benefits and hence the 'Worth' of the SubStrategy both globally and to each stakeholder. Many books and articles have been written on the subject of determining the Worth of Benefits. This Wikipedia page https://en.wikipedia.org/wiki/Cost%E2%80%93benefit_analysis is a good place to find many relevant articles so we will not go into details here. The key point is that the beneficiaries of the Benefits will have the clearest perspective on the Worth of the Benefits – so ask them!

a.   Global Worth: Determine if the consolidated Worth of all the Benefits exceed the total costs of all the Projects plus the total costs of all the Uses. If the Worth of the Benefits exceeds the combined costs of the Projects and Uses, then the SubStrategy is 'Globally Worth it', mathematically: $\Sigma W_B \geq (\Sigma C_P + \Sigma C_U)$ where

i. ΣW_B is the total Worth of the Benefits (economic, social, environmental, cultural);

ii. ΣC_P is the total cost of all the Projects;

iii. ΣC_U is the total cost of all the Uses.

b.   Motivational Worth: Determine if the combined Worths of the Benefits to each stakeholder are sufficient to motivate that stakeholder to contribute as required to the SubStrategy. In particular, determine if the Worth to the users is sufficient to motivate their Uses.

In real-world situations, Worths and costs include a mixture of economic, social, environmental and cultural Worths, so the determination of Global Worth is challenging – challenging but not impossible, at least semi-quantitatively. The non-financial Global Worths determination is likely to be more of a narrative in which the Worths of the Benefits are compared with the costs of the Projects and Uses. So for example, riparian planting may improve water quality, enabling fauna and flora to thrive and generate robust ecosystem health (Worthwhile Benefits which may be difficult to translate into economic terms) while reducing nutrient availability for aquaculture (a cost that would be relatively easy to translate into economic terms).

The key point in this stage is that these Worths and costs have been *explicitly identified* and quantified *in their own terms (not necessarily financial)*, so are available for the next stage (Stage 5: Making investment decisions) in which the stakeholders need to apply their respective weightings on the *relative* Worth/costs of economic, social, environmental and cultural factors.

4.   If necessary, upgrade the SubStrategy so that:

a.   It will produce sufficient Global Worth.

b.   It will produce sufficient Motivational Worth for each and every key stakeholder.

c.   As a minimum, 'sufficient Global Worth' means that the Worth of the Benefits exceeds the costs of the Projects and Uses. However, 'sufficient' for investing in a SubStrategy may apply a higher standard such as 'more sufficient than competing SubStrategies'. Each SubStrategy needs to be made as attractive as possible by identifying and quantifying Benefits and Worths that are already inherent in the SubStrategy but which might not yet have been made clear. It also means modifying the SubStrategy to improve the quality and quantity of the Benefits and Worth. Often this can be done relatively easily, especially by identifying additional low-cost Uses which will generate Worthwhile new Benefits or Benefits for new stakeholders.

d.   If the Motivational Worth to any stakeholder is insufficient then the SubStrategy will need to be improved to increase that Worth so that the individual stakeholders are sufficiently motivated to play their part. This may mean improving or adding new Projects, Results, Uses and Benefits so as to achieve both Global Worth and Motivational Worth for all stakeholders. If necessary, upgrade the SubStrategy so that it will produce sufficient Global and Motivational Worth for all key stakeholders and/or check to see if some Project or Uses are particularly expensive and determine what would happen if they were modified or eliminated. Sometimes a relatively minor change in a SubStrategy can have a profound impact on whether or not the SubStrategy is Globally or Motivationally 'Worth it'.

e. Determining Motivational Worth and if it is sufficient for all stakeholders involves checking with each key stakeholder to determine if they feel sufficiently motivated by the Worth they will derive to contribute as required to implementing the SubStrategy.

5. If the SubStrategy is compelling in terms of Global Worth but it is not compelling in terms of Motivational Worth for some stakeholders then, *as a last resort*, consider if some form of regulation or coercion can be applied to 'encourage' those stakeholders to contribute as required to implementing the SubStrategy. Such coercion could be regulations with penalties for non-compliance together with effective enforcements. Other forms of coercion might include public and peer pressure.

6. Identify those performance indicators and targets associated with each Project, Result, Use and Benefit that will provide both lead and lag information on costs and Worth. Stages 1 to 3 *identified* relevant indicators but they didn't *quantify* them. So for example, include indicators and targets that will:

a. Quantify the costs to each Project stakeholder *as well as* quantifying the *number* of such stakeholders in order to determine the consolidated costs of all Projects including economic, social, environmental and cultural costs.

b. Quantify the costs to each user *as well as* quantifying the *number* of Uses and *frequency and duration* of Uses in order to determine the consolidated costs of all Uses including economic, social, environmental and cultural costs.

c. Quantify the Worth of the Benefits to each recipient *as well as* quantifying the *number* of such participants in order to determine the consolidated and individual Benefits to each and every stakeholder. Such Worths include economic, social, environmental and cultural Worths.

Demonstration of Stage 4 actions

Let us now use the hypothetical Pingo River water quality SubStrategy to illustrate this Stage 4. Figure 7.2 shows what this hypothetical and simplistic SubStrategy looks like after the first 3 stages.

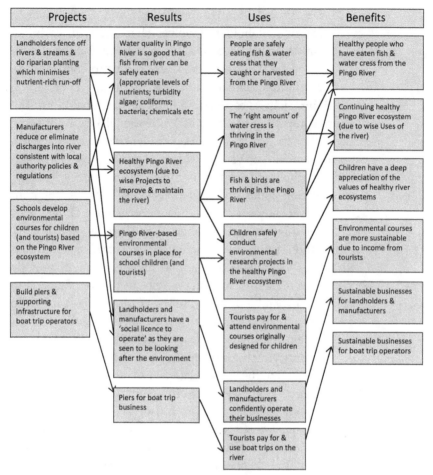

Figure 7.2   Aspirational-level SubStrategy on environmentally sound Uses of the hypothetical Pingo River.

1.   Identify, quantify and add up the costs of each Project:
      Many of the financial costs of the Projects will be easy to determine, e.g. the cost of installing fencing; planting riparian-strip plants; installing pollution control devices in factories; developing environmental courses; building piers.
      Other costs may be less obvious but could include:
      a.   loss of time/increased costs to landowners through no longer being able to ford waterways across their property and having to use a limited number of bridges;

b.   loss of recreational access to the Pingo River due to fencing, especially tall deer fencing, and dense riparian plantings such as large flaxes;

c.   the cost of disposal of concentrated pollutants that have been collected within the industrial pollution control systems;

d.   loss of community cohesion if landholders feel resentment at being coerced into fencing and riparian planting;

e.   loss of a social licence to operate if landholders are seen as continuing to cause water pollution problems;

f.   loss of productivity in Pingo River and downstream marine aquaculture due to fewer nutrients (pollution) from run-off from land (this is an actual example from mussel farming in the Marlborough Sounds in New Zealand);

g.   loss of free recreational access to riverbanks where commercial piers are installed (conversely, if the piers are available for public use then such Uses may generate real Worth for some stakeholders such as boaties).

Many of these costs will not only be difficult to identify but also difficult to quantify in financial terms. This is where it is imperative to engage with all stakeholders and ask *them* to identify and quantify (financially, where possible) all costs that they might incur in association with Projects. Costs which cannot be readily quantified financially should be recorded as narratives and used to help inform decision making in Stage 5.

2.   Identify, quantify and add up the true costs to each user of each Use and multiply by the number of users and frequency of Uses:

Many of the financial costs of the Uses will be easy to determine, for example the cost of catching fish and harvesting watercress; the cost of getting schoolchildren to and from the Pingo River; the costs to tourists of attending the environmental courses.

Other costs may be less obvious but could include:

a.   increased costs to consumers of agricultural or manufactured products;

b.   ecosystem disruption such as water-bird nesting disturbance due to commercial boat trips on the waterways;

c.   the disruption to fishing and watercress harvesting due to commercial boat trips;

d.   ecosystem damage due to petrochemical pollutants leaking from boats;

e.   loss of peaceful enjoyment of the Pingo River by people living along the riverbanks due to the constant passage of commercial boat tours.

As with Project costs, many of these Use costs will not only be difficult to identify but also difficult to quantify in financial terms. This is where it is imperative to engage with all stakeholders and ask *them* to identify and quantify (financially, where possible) all costs that they might incur in association with Uses. Costs which cannot be readily quantified financially should be recorded as narratives and used to help inform decision making in Stage 5.

3.   Determine the Global and Motivational Worth of the Benefits and hence the 'Worth' of the SubStrategy both globally and to each stakeholder:

Consider the Worth of the five Benefits in the Pingo River SubStrategy.

- Healthy and happy people who have eaten fish and watercress from the Pingo River.
- Continuing healthy Pingo River ecosystem (due to wise Uses of the river).
- Children have a deep appreciation of the Worth of healthy river ecosystems.
- Environmental courses are more sustainable due to income from tourists.
- Sustainable businesses for boat trip operators.
  a.   The fourth and fifth Benefits are straightforward economic Benefits that will be easy to determine so will not be discussed here. In contrast, Benefits 1–3 will be more challenging because they are primarily social, environmental and cultural.
  b.   The first Benefit of: healthy people who have eaten fish and watercress from the Pingo River: on first glance this appears to be a 'health' Benefit and certainly health is a key element of this Benefit. However, how many people will

actually gain this Benefit and how often will they do so? Experience shows that in such situations, many people want 'to *be able* to eat fish and water from the river' but in reality few will actually *do* so.

c. So, perhaps a better wording of this Benefit would be: "People are happy knowing that other people are demonstrably safely eating fish and watercress from the river and that they would also be healthy if they also ate fish and watercress from the river". So in this instance, the Worth derives primarily from '*knowing* that the fish and watercress are safe to eat' and less so from actually eating them.

d. How big is this Worth? Ask the people who say it is important to them. Currently (2019) in New Zealand, there are strong demands for our waterways to be cleaned up so they can be safely swum in or food can be harvested from them. This issue was a major factor in the 2017 parliamentary and 2019 local government elections and contributed to the election of a more demonstrably pro-environment government, so it clearly has great Worth to many people who see it as a non-negotiable bottom-line. This has high Worth in an election year!

e. This Benefit is a perfect example of a Benefit that was originally slightly misworded and in which people place a Worth on 'knowing they would be healthy if they did something' rather than actually doing that something. This does not necessarily reduce the Worth of the Benefit because people often place a high Worth on being *able* to do something even if they do not actually *do* it. (Similarly, people will often fight to be allowed to vote democratically but when they actually have the right to vote, many people do not exercise it).

f. Let us now consider the second Benefit: Continuing healthy Pingo River ecosystem (due to wise Uses of the river). This Benefit is primarily an environmental Benefit but, like the first Benefit, is something that many people want as a matter of principle rather than because they will personally experience that Benefit. Many people get pleasure from knowing that fish, birds, insects and plants are thriving in their local rivers and are upset, and may become politically active, when river ecosystems degrade even if they never visit the river. Also, the species living in the river are able to create Benefits by using the cleaner river as their homes, even if few people visit the rivers. In addition, many cultures place a high spiritual or cultural Value on clean water, so this Benefit encapsulates environmental Worth, social Worth and cultural Worth.

g.   How big are these Worths? They are similar to the first Benefit in that for many people they are non-negotiable bottom-lines that they will continue to fight for in the political arena. To those who want these Benefits they are highly valued, but to many other people they are not all that important. The tourism industry may argue strongly that these ecosystem-health Worths support the financial sustainability of that industry. In contrast, high intensity, irrigating dairy farmers may argue that such Benefits are insignificant compared to the financial Benefits of an industry that generates significant export earnings and hence increased wealth for society. They may also argue that dairying has been a binding force in communities for generations, so has added substantial social and cultural Worth.

h.   Associated with this Benefit are economic Worth; environmental Worth; social Worth and cultural Worth; all of which need to be identified and at least semi-quantified in order to determine both Global Worth and Motivational Worth for this SubStrategy.

     i.   The third Benefit: children have a deep apprecia-
tion of the Worth of healthy river ecosystems is
an interesting one in that it is unlikely to motivate most children although it may motivate
many parents and teachers. Having said that, a
significant number of children will indeed put
a significant Worth on this Benefit once they
are older and have a deeper appreciation of the
world. So, the Benefit accrues to the children but
the Motivational Worth of that Benefit accrues
initially to their parents and teachers and only
in later years to the children (remembering that
this is a hypothetical example to illustrate the
nature of Benefits and their associated Global
and Motivational Worth).

This example SubStrategy demonstrates a truism of most
strategies: that the Worths and costs arise from a mixture
of economic, social, environmental and cultural factors.
Because different stakeholders evaluate these Benefits and
Worth differently, there will be no single master-list of high-
priority SubStrategies but rather there will be different sets
of SubStrategies that will be high priority to different groups
of stakeholders. If progress is to be made and actions taken,
stakeholders will need to understand each other's Motivational
and Global Worths and invariably make some compromises
so that all parties gain sufficient Benefits to motivate them to
play their part in making the strategy work.

Stage 5 in the PRUB 9-stage process (Chapter 8) discusses how such divergences of priorities can be addressed
collaboratively.

Once the Worth of the Benefits and the costs of the Projects
and Uses have been collected and documented in meaningful terms (a challenging task!), it is then a relatively simple
mathematical calculation to determine the Global Worth if all
the Worth and costs have been converted into financial terms,
i.e.: if $\Sigma W_B \geq (\Sigma C_P + \Sigma C_U)$. This may mean weighing up the
values of social Benefits against economic or environmental
Benefits and this often becomes a 'political' discussion. If it
has not been possible to translate all of the costs and Benefits
into financial terms, they will just have to be recorded and

used semi-objectively in Stage 5: Making investment decisions. The key point in Stage 4 is that Worth and costs have been *explicitly identified* and quantified *in their own terms (not necessarily financial)*, so are available for Stage 5 in which the stakeholders need to apply their respective weightings on the *relative* Worths/costs of economic, social, environmental and cultural factors.

4. If necessary, upgrade the SubStrategy so that:

    a. It will produce sufficient Global Worth.

        i. As a minimum, 'sufficient Global Worth' means that the Worth of the Benefits exceeds the combined costs of the Projects and Uses. So for example, as the Pingo River is restored it may, at minimal cost, become attractive to canoeists, wild-life photographers and picnickers. Inclusion of additional Valuable Benefits and associated Uses may give the overall SubStrategy a greater Global Worth

    b. It will produce sufficient Motivational Worth for each and every key stakeholder.

        i. In this example of the Pingo River in its current form, there appear to be minimal Benefits or Worth to landholders or manufacturers of minimising nutrient run-off and discharge of industrial pollutants into the river.

        ii. While it could be tempting to legislate that landholders/manufacturers *must* minimise pollution into the river (or risk incurring significant penalties), this may not be the best approach at this point in the process. It is better to determine if there are in fact Worthwhile Benefits that landholders/manufacturers could gain from their pollution-minimisation efforts and to only use coercion as a last resort and/or find ways to minimise or share the pollution-reducing Project costs.

        iii. What Valuable Benefits might the landholders/manufacturers gain from better management of their nutrients/pollutants? In New Zealand, many farmers are changing their land Uses because the loss of nutrients reduces farm productivity. Such land-use changes lead to lower demands for fertilisers, higher crop and animal yields and cleaner and more fishable rivers running through the farmer's own land – all of which generate Worth for the farmers and their families.

iv. Further, those landholders who are reducing their nutrient run-off are strengthening their 'social licence to operate'.

v. So, while such improved land management practices are far from universal, a significant number of farmers *are motivated* by the Worth to them of these Benefits so they do not need coercion.

vi. Instead of increasing the Worth of the Benefits, it may be best to reduce or redistribute Project and Use costs so as to increase the net Motivational Worth for affected stakeholders. This may be achieved through government grants, crowd-funding or by other stakeholders offering to freely contribute their time, e.g. for helping farmers with riparian planting or weed control.

5. If sufficiently compelling Motivational Worth cannot be created then, *as a last resort*, consider if some form of regulation or coercion can be applied to 'encourage' those stakeholders to contribute as required to implementing the SubStrategy:

a. Some landowners (including government agencies) may remain unmotivated by saving nutrient costs, improving productivity and strengthening their social licence to operate. In this instance, and as a last resort, authorities with responsibility for water quality may use coercive legislation to 'encourage' those farmers to contribute to the restoration of degraded rivers such as the hypothetical Pingo River.

6. Identify those performance indicators and targets associated with each Project, Result, Use and Benefit that will provide both lead and lag information on costs and Worth. The following examples relate to the Pingo River SubStrategy:

a.   An indicator for 'healthy people' might include the number of hospital admissions for people who have consumed food from the river (a measure of 'un-health') with a target that this must be fewer than one every 5 years. This is not a very useful indicator because it will have a very small data set and will only measure extremes of un-health rather than 'healthy people'. Also, it may be that everyone knew the river was unhealthy so no-one consumed food from it historically, so there may be no base-line data set. However it would be easy to measure and translate this indicator into economic Worth, so it could be tempting to use this indicator.

b.   A better indicator for 'healthy people' might come from surveys of the rates of gastrointestinal illnesses of regular consumers of food from the river (e.g. the local indigenous population). This is a slightly better indicator as it will contain more data on more minor levels of un-health but again, it is measuring un-health, not health and as with 6a it may have no base-line data set if everyone has been avoiding what they knew to be a polluted river.

c.   So, an even better indicator for 'healthy people' might be the number of regular consumers of food from the river who report that they feel good consuming the food and also for several days thereafter with a target of 99% saying this. This is a meaningful indicator and target which would definitely confirm (or not) if the SubStrategy was being implemented effectively.

d.   Indicators and targets for 'healthy Pingo River ecosystem' might include: the number of nesting birds; the density of fish and invertebrates; the distribution and local density of watercress; the frequency of blooms of blue-green algae and the levels of faecal coliforms.

e.   Indicators and targets for 'children with a deep appreciation of the River' might include the number of children who sign-up for a subsequent series of river restoration Projects with a target of 10%.

Accountabilities in Stage 4

1. Because the *nature* of the Benefits has already been deter-
    mined in Stages 1–3, the accountabilities in this stage relate to
    quantifying:
    a. Global Worth;
    b. Motivational Worth.
    Both of which depend on quantifying
    c. Project costs;
    d. Use costs.
2. Responsibilities:
    a. Quantifying the Global and Motivational Worth of the
        SubStrategies is *primarily* the responsibility of the pur-
        chasers but will necessarily depend heavily on obtain-
        ing accurately quantified information from users on
        the Worth of the Benefits to them and to others.
    b. Quantifying Project Efficiency with which Projects
        create Results is *primarily* the responsibility of the
        suppliers.
    c. Quantifying the Use Efficiency with which Uses gener-
        ate Benefits is *primarily* the responsibility of purchasers
        and will require accurately quantitative information
        from end-users.

Comments

1. It can appear challenging to determine the Worth of Benefits,
    especially of non-financial Benefits (social, environmental,
    cultural).
2. While non-financial Benefits have inherent Worths, it is a sad
    fact of life that many strategy investment decisions are based
    on financial Worth alone.
3. For any SubStrategy with modest financial Benefits (or even
    losses) it will increase the chances of the SubStrategy being
    funded if the Worths of social, environmental and cultural
    Benefits can be at least semi-quantified in financial terms.
    This is a non-ideal but also pragmatic step until such time that
    investment decisions are less-finance-driven and are more
    inspired by the Worths of all four well-beings.

4.   The beneficiaries of the Benefits will have the clearest per-
      spective on Benefits and their Worths – so ask them! Stage 1
      (engaging with end-users) *identified* the Benefits and poten-
      tially *identified* how end-users might determine the Worth of
      those Benefits. This Stage 4 needs to go further to:

      a.   determine the Worths of those Benefits in terms of the
            4 well-beings;

      b.   translate the non-financial Worths into financial
            Worths where this is possible, solely because invest-
            ment decisions are so often based primarily on finan-
            cial considerations.

5.   The costs of the Uses *must* always be taken into account
      because very often the ongoing costs of the Uses far exceed
      the upfront and/or ongoing costs of the Projects. A classic
      example is the amalgamation of multiple local hospitals into
      a single regional hospital. The costs of establishing and run-
      ning one hospital (Projects) are lower than the costs of estab-
      lishing and running many hospitals (Projects). However, the
      cumulative costs to all the users of travelling to a central hos-
      pital and potentially having to stay overnight can be much
      larger than the savings in the establishment and running of
      a single regional hospital. Importantly, *taxpayers are paying all
      the costs in both cases – and in fact with the centralised hospital, the
      costs to the users fall primarily on sick people*! It becomes a politi-
      cal decision whether or not it is better to run more expen-
      sive local hospitals that make visiting the hospital cheaper
      for sick and disadvantaged people, or to run a single, cheaper
      regional hospital that disproportionately loads the Use costs
      onto the sick people.

6.   Do not make investment decisions in this stage. It is important
      to complete this stage so that all stakeholders are crystal clear
      about the *potential* Benefits, and the Global and Motivational
      Worths of each SubStrategy. As a consequence, different
      stakeholders will have different levels of enthusiasm for each
      SubStrategy so that in Stage 5 where SubStrategies are priori-
      tised, it is likely that some SubStrategies that are seen as low
      priority by some stakeholders will be seen as high priority by
      other stakeholders. Most importantly, it may be that there is
      more than one source of funds and resources to support each
      SubStrategy, so in the next stage, different SubStrategies may

be (sometimes unexpectedly) funded/resourced by different stakeholders.

7.   Some stakeholders such as suppliers will be paid for their services so in effect that payment is a Result. However, in this world of increased accountability, such payment will ideally be tied to the *effectiveness* of the Results in 'enabling and motivating Uses to create Benefits'. Since such effectiveness will only be known *after* the Uses have happened, this book will recognise payment to suppliers as Benefits to the suppliers, rather than as Results. In this sense, PRUB-Logic makes it crystal clear that Benefits are not Results – that it is solely Benefits that have Worth whereas Results embody costs: even if they are outstandingly good Results they still embody costs to the SubStrategy. So, a purchaser 'loses Worth' when they pay money to a supplier while the end-users (who often fund the purchaser through taxes and commercial payments) 'gain Worth' from using the infrastructure, goods and services that the supplier provides.

8.   In our experience, far too often a lot of effort is put into Stages 1–4 (end-user engagement, supplier engagement; strategising; creating business cases) at which point the process stops because no-one is prepared to commit to making binding decisions that may require new resources or require the reallocation of resources from existing activities. This is an unfortunate reality in this world. However, by having succinct, convincingly *Validated* SubStrategies and business cases, it makes it easier for stakeholders to make investment decisions (Stage 5) and convince their constituents that the decisions are good ones.

Once you have quantified Global and Motivational Worths of Benefits and identified if/where coercion may be necessary, then you are ready to move to Stage 5 – making investment decisions about Validated SubStrategies (Chapter 8).

Chapter 8

Stage 5 – Make investment decisions

Reminder: Our purpose is *to enable and motivate Uses to create Benefits*

PRUB Mantra #1: *Only Uses create Benefits*

PRUB Mantra #2: Uses need the *right* Results or they won't happen

PRUB Mantra #3: Projects, Results, Uses and Benefits must be Linked with compelling Evidence

PRUB Mantra #4: SubStrategies must be Globally and Motivationally Worth it

PRUB Mantra #5: Invest in the 'best' SubStrategies

What is Stage 5?

Stage 5 will produce a robust, defensible and prioritised set of SubStrategies that have been approved for investment. Ideally, each SubStrategy will be accompanied by a *PRUB Validation Index* which provides scores for the quality of the three elements of validation:

The *PRUB Validation Index* is a set of 3 numbers which represent:

1. how logical the SubStrategy is (on a score of 1–5);
2. how strong the Evidence for all the Links in the SubStrategy is (on a score of 1–5);
3. how Worthwhile the SubStrategy is (on a score of 1–5).

Stage 5 consists of comparing multiple *Validated* SubStrategies (SubStrategies that are simultaneously logical; Evidence-based; and both Globally and Motivationally Worth it) and selecting those that best fit the investment criteria of the various decision makers as determined in Stage 1.

The PRUB-Logic approach in Stage 5 will enable and encourage subgroups to operate independently by implementing their own strategies; and simultaneously cooperatively, by fully recognising all other SubStrategies and how they interlink with their own SubStrategy. They will therefore operate collaboratively in such a manner that the overall Worth of the Benefits is greater than the sum of the Benefits from the individual SubStrategies (Global Worth). The PRUB-Logic approach will also take into consideration the crucial need for each and every stakeholder to be motivated (Motivational Worth) to make their necessary contributions. The PRUB-Logic approach enables each subgroup to retain ownership, responsibility, accountability and motivation for their own decisions and budgets while still 'joining up' (not 'pooling') their budgets (see *Validating Strategies*, pages 142–143).

What Stage 5 will achieve in order to support the other 8 stages

1.   General investments: a prioritised list of SubStrategies that *decision-making* stakeholders have *collectively* agreed to invest in.

2.   Subgroup Investments: Sets of other SubStrategies that other *decision-making* individuals or subgroups of stakeholders have agreed to invest in even if these SubStrategies are not universally supported by all stakeholders (see Figure 8.1).

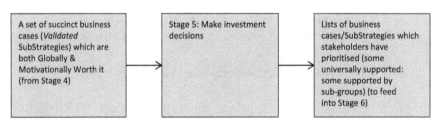

Figure 8.1   The precursor to Stage 5, Stage 5 itself and what Stage 5 must feed into Stage 6.

WHY IS STAGE 5 IMPORTANT?

1. Almost invariably there will not be enough resources to implement all potential SubStrategies, so it is necessary to select 'the best ones'.

2. The best ones will be those that, as a minimum:

   a. are the most *Validated* (having the highest *PRUB Validation Index* scores for being logical; Evidence-based and Globally and Motivationally Worth it);

   b. meet other criteria (affordability; social acceptability; political acceptability and so on).

3. Simultaneously:

   a. some SubStrategies are likely to gain investment from most if not all of a group of stakeholders;

   b. other SubStrategies may gain investment from subgroups who strongly support such SubStrategies even if they are not supported by the totality of stakeholders;

   c. occasionally some SubStrategies will be prohibited because although they are strongly supported by a subgroup of stakeholders they will have too many negative impacts on other stakeholders for them to be acceptable.

4. So, politics enters at this point as the stakeholders determine the *relative* Worth of each of the 4 well-beings for the entire group of stakeholders and/or for subgroups of stakeholders.

5. What is likely to emerge from this decision-making stage is several lists of SubStrategies that have attracted enough investment so that they can be implemented. The SubStrategies will be prioritised by different groups of stakeholders according to different weightings of costs and Benefits, depending on, for example:

   a. the nature and Worth of the Benefits (economic; social, environmental; cultural);

   b. the potential for the simultaneous implementation of several SubStrategies to complement each other;

   c. the identities of the beneficiaries of the Benefits;

   d. the investment costs (money, other resources);

   e. who will fund or provide resources for each SubStrategy;

   f. the political acceptability of the SubStrategies which may create both Benefits and dis-Benefits;

   g. the suppliers who will lead the Projects;

   h. the probability that the SubStrategies can actually be implemented (dependent on how compelling the cause-and-effect Evidence is within each SubStrategy).

6. For example, some stakeholder groups may place a high Worth on economic return and a low Worth on the environment whereas other groups may take the opposite approach.

7. This means that it is often the case that different subgroups have a different priority order for the potential SubStrategies.

8. So, in the real world there is seldom a 'single list of priorities' but rather there are distinctly separate lists of priorities for each group or subgroup – *and that is OK!*

9. By basing initial investment decisions (or, as a minimum, the triaging of options) on SubStrategies, it becomes clear where the political preferences are being applied.

10. When making investment decisions, fully *Validated* SubStrategies are easy to compare with each other because they use the same simple language and logical constructs to define the SubStrategies. They also take a consistent approach to *identifying* those costs and Benefits that matter to stakeholders, even if they take divergent approaches to determining the *Worth* of those Benefits. It may mean that in many instances it will be necessary to compare SubStrategies having high financial Worth with SubStrategies that have low financial Worth but have high environmental or social or cultural Worth. This is the reality of life and it is not easy making these comparisons. The key point here is that the format of SubStrategies makes these comparisons *as clear and explicit as it is possible to be*, by using 'the smallest amount of strategic information that has the highest value to the most people'.

11. So while it may be necessary to conduct full Better Business Case or Investment Logic Mapping investigations before making any specific investment in order to take into account all possible ways of assessing and valuing a SubStrategy, *Validated* SubStrategies are nevertheless excellent for triaging and short listing preferred SubStrategies.

Summary of the start-to-finish action sequence for Stage 5

1.   Stakeholder groups and subgroups establish their own standards for the *relative* Worth of economic, social, environmental and cultural Global and Motivational Worth.

2.   Check that these relative Worths align with, or at least achieve a reasonable balance of, the group's agreed overall Values and Fundamental Principles from Stage 1.

3.   Check that each business case (*Validated SubStrategy*) is fully *Validated* in the context of the newly determined *relative* Worths.

4.   Determine the 3-digit *PRUB Validation Index* for each SubStrategy, i.e. the 3 numbers which represent:

   a.   how logical the SubStrategy is (on a score of 1–5);

   b.   how strong the Evidence for all the Links in the SubStrategy is (on a score of 1–5);

   c.   how Worthwhile the SubStrategy is (on a score of 1–5).

5.   Prioritise investments in SubStrategies using the 3-step process recommended in *Validating Strategies*, pages 105–108:

   a.   voting;

   b.   clustering of subgroups around preferred SubStrategies;

   c.   clustering or blending of SubStrategies into new SubStrategies that are worth implementing.

6.   For major SubStrategies, probably undertake more comprehensive analyses using methods such as Better Business Case:

   https://treasury.govt.nz/information-and-services/state-sector-leadership/investment-management/better-business-cases/guidance

   or Investment Logic Mapping:

   https://treasury.govt.nz/information-and-services/state-sector-leadership/better-business-cases-bbc/bbc-methods-and-tools/investment-logic-mapping

7.   Reconfirm the most relevant performance indicators and associated targets associated with each Project, Result, Use and Benefit so that they can be used to monitor the agreed priority Worths.

Explanation of the start-to-finish action sequence for Stage 5

1.   Stakeholder groups and subgroups establish their own standards for the *relative* Worth of economic, social, environmental and cultural Global and Motivational Worths:

   a.   Each stakeholder group and subgroup must agree on their own priorities for the *relative* Worth of economic, social, environmental and cultural Benefits to the stakeholder group and/or to subgroups and individuals even if these priorities differ from subgroup to subgroup.

b.   It is entirely appropriate for subgroups to prioritise their own Worths differently from other subgroups while acknowledging that in a multi-stakeholder environment some compromises may be necessary. However, such compromises can in the long term generate win-win situations such as where the long-term viabilities of both businesses and the environment can be achieved (see example below in relation to the rejuvenation of a CBD).

c.   So, rather than attempting to get everyone to agree on the same priorities for Global and Motivational Worth, it is much healthier and more realistic to guide stakeholders to negotiate ways in which their differing Worth-priorities can be complementary rather than competitive.

2.   Check that these relative Worths align with, or strike a fair balance of, the group's agreed overall Values and Fundamental Principles:

a.   The Global and Motivation Worths generated in Stage 4 will probably have altered the stakeholder group's and subgroups' perceptions of overall Values and Fundamental Principles from Stage 1.

b.   At this point stakeholders should refer back to the original Values and Fundamental Principles and either update them to align with the Global and Motivational Worths or alternatively revise the Global and Motivational Worths so that they align with the original Values and Fundamental Principles.

c.   It is likely that the Global and Motivational Worths will be strongly correlated with on the ground reality as they will have been derived from *actual* SubStrategies that have been *Validated*, rather than being an initial set of idealised Values and Fundamental Principles which were developed before the detailed SubStrategies emerged. It is therefore recommended that generally the ground-truthed Global and Motivational Worths should guide the refinement of the earlier statements of Value and Fundamental Principles rather than the other way around.

d.   This step within Stage 5 therefore requires stakeholders to correlate the idealism of the initial Values and Fundamental Principles with the realism of the Global and Motivational Worths. This can be a particularly soul-searching exercise as idealism confronts pragmatism. However, this step is essential in order to keep stakeholders' perspectives correlated as much as possible with the emerging *Validated* SubStrategies which will soon be implemented.

3.   Check that each business case (*Validated SubStrategy*) is fully *Validated* in the context of the newly determined *relative Worths* including both full-group Worths and subgroup Worths:

a.   As Worths are reconsidered in this stage it often becomes clear that the Motivational Worths *to specific key stakeholders (e.g. end-users)* are recognised as being more significant than first thought and may now require the enabling of more/different Uses to generate more Worthwhile Benefits for those stakeholders.

b.   For example, a SubStrategy may have been fully *financially Validated* in Stage 4 but if social or cultural Worths are now considered pre-eminent in this Stage 5, then the same SubStrategy may *not be socially or culturally Validated*

c.   So, as SubStrategies and Worth-priorities emerge and evolve it is essential to check and recheck the *Validation* of the SubStrategies and update them if necessary, especially if the potential investors and end-users have different Worth-priorities from those of the rest of the stakeholders.

4.   Determine the 3-digit *Validation Index* for each SubStrategy:

a.   the *PRUB Validation Index* is a set of 3 numbers which represent:

i.   how logical the SubStrategy is (*PRUB-Logic* on a score of 1–5);

ii.   how strong the Evidence for all the Links in the SubStrategy is (*PRUB-Evidence* on a score of 1–5);

iii.   how Worthwhile the SubStrategy is (*PRUB-Worth* on a score of 1–5).

b.   The *PRUB Validation Index* is a concept that is still under development in order to make it as objective as possible. At the moment we rely on human judgement to determine the scores for each of the three *PRUB-Validation* criteria.

c.   The key point is that each of the three criteria should at least be considered carefully. Some attempt should be made to put a semi-quantitative number on each criterion because even subjectively, it is usually clear that some SubStrategies are *more* logical and *more* Evidence-based and *more* Worthwhile than others.

d.   If the *PRUB-Logic* score is low, then the subsequent *PRUB-Evidence* and *PRUB-Worth* scores must also be low because they are dependent on robust *PRUB-Logic*. Similarly, if the *PRUB-Evidence* score is low, then the *PRUB-Worth* score must also be low because there will be a low level of confidence that the correct factors have been taken into account in determining the *PRUB-Worth* of a SubStrategy.

e.   Readers of this book are encouraged to contribute their perspectives on the *PRUB Validation Index* to phil@openstrategies.com.

5.   Prioritise investments in SubStrategies using the 3-step process recommended in *Validating Strategies*, pages 105–108 and summarised here:

a.   **Simple voting**: There are various voting methods that can work such as the chosen decision-making stakeholders each having a set number of 'points' that they can allocate to their preferred SubStrategies and then the SubStrategies prioritised based on the number of points they were given. Simple voting identifies *the least controversial* SubStrategies which are not necessarily the *best* SubStrategies or the SubStrategies that are the *most important to subgroups*.

b.   **Clustering of subgroups**: Often, subgroups of stakeholders collectively place a high Worth on certain SubStrategies/business cases. This identifies *SubStrategies that are important to subgroups* but not necessarily to the whole group. If the subgroup is big enough and sufficiently resourced and their desired

SubStrategies do not cause problems for other stakeholders, then perhaps the subgroup can find their own
funding and resources and 'get on with it'.

c.   **Clustering/combining of SubStrategies**: It is often possible to combine or consolidate several SubStrategies
which each have limited stakeholder support, into *a*
single combined/modified SubStrategy which has sufficient
stakeholder support to attract resources and funds to
make it happen.

Letting go of some SubStrategies: consistent with the limited resources in most situations, some SubStrategies will
not proceed and this may seriously upset some stakeholders. Ideally other stakeholders will be sensitive to this situation and will endeavour to accommodate some of the
non-funded SubStrategies' Uses and Benefits into the funded
SubStrategies.

6.   For major SubStrategies, it is probably best to undertake
more comprehensive analyses using methods such as Better
Business Case (BBC) or Investment Logic Mapping (ILM) (see
links identified earlier in this chapter) to confirm the merits,
and the relative merits in the eyes of each stakeholder, of each
business case:

a.   This additional analysis may come after or before the
previous prioritisation stage depending on the level of
confidence in the Validity of the succinct SubStrategy-
based business cases.

b.   A robustly Validated SubStrategy or suite of interlinked SubStrategies provide much of the core starting
information necessary for BBC or ILM.

c.   In this situation it may be appropriate to integrate all
the SubStrategies (which is straightforward to do if
they are all in the common PRUB-Logic format) so that
stakeholders have a clear understanding of what the
full suite of approved SubStrategies will enable and
create.

d.   BBC and ILM are likely to identify new issues that will
need to be absorbed into the SubStrategies on a case by
case basis.

e.   The key point here is that SubStrategies provide a succinct business case for strategic ideas which enables

them to be quickly compared and prioritised (triaged) in order to select a short-list for more detailed analysis using more comprehensive – and more expensive – techniques.

7. Reconfirm the most relevant performance indicators and associated targets associated with each Project, Result, Use and Benefit so that they can be used to monitor the agreed priority Worths and Values:

a. The first step in this Stage 5 (confirm relative Worths of economic, social, environmental and cultural Worths) may shift the emphasis from, for example, economic to social Worth, or from social to environmental or cultural Worth so it is possible, even likely, that the previously identified indicators and targets will no longer be ideal.

b. While necessary for project and logistical management, previously chosen financial indicators and targets may no longer be sufficient for monitoring and managing environmental, social or cultural values. New ones will need to be identified and quantified prior to Stage 6 (preparation of contracts) in order to quantify performance against these values.

Demonstration of Stage 5 actions

Let us now consider these Stage 5 actions in the context of local government leading the redevelopment of a declining suburban Central Business District (CBD). Stages 1 to 4 produced the hypothetical Aspirational-level SubStrategy shown in Figure 8.2.

This Aspirational-level SubStrategy has identified just a few of the many characteristics of the redevelopment of a hypothetical CBD. A large interlinked collection of detailed SubStrategies would be required to create an effective overall strategy. For example, there would need to be SubStrategies on parking, public transport, environmental management, education, health, public safety, visitor and tourist accommodation, recreational activities and so on. Each such SubStrategy would be in exactly the same PRUB-format as this Aspirational-level strategy and this would make it easy to interlink all the various SubStrategies with each other.

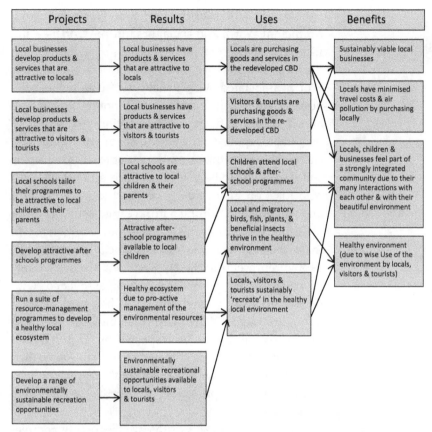

Figure 8.2 **Aspirational SubStrategy for the redevelopment of a declining suburban Central Business District (CBD).**

There would invariably be some negative Links such as a Use of "Local and migratory birds ... thrive in a healthy environment" causing a negative link to 'Healthy environment' due to the effluent that large numbers of birds create (see *Validating Strategies*, page 34 for a discussion of negative links in SubStrategies).

Given these provisos, let us now look at how the steps in Stage 5 would work with this example.

1. Stakeholder groups and subgroups establish their own standards for the *relative Worths* of economic, social, environmental and cultural Global and Motivational Worths:
    a. Even at this high-level, low-detail Aspirational SubStrategy it is clear that different elements of this

SubStrategy will prioritise economic Worth over environmental Worth and social or cultural Worths – and vice versa.

b.   Business leaders are likely to prioritise economic Worth associated with Benefit #1: 'sustainable businesses'. Their prioritisation of economic Worth will almost certainly be an absolute bottom-line and non-negotiable because if the businesses are not financially sustainable then they simply cannot exist, so this perspective needs to be respected. Such economic-Worth prioritisation may initially be short-to-medium term and may involve 'mining natural capital' such as using up finite resources which, once they are gone, will make the businesses no longer financially sustainable.

c.   People representing the environment are more likely to prioritise environmental Worth associated with Benefit #4: 'healthy environment'. Their prioritisation of environmental Worth will often be a strongly held perspective and must be respected but if it can only be achieved in a financially non-sustainable way, then some compromises may be required.

d.   These differing priorities of Worths are entirely reasonable!

e.   Differing priorities of Worths are frequently complementary. For example, a healthy environment is likely to attract more people to the CBD which will enhance the financial sustainability of the businesses. Financial sustainability in turn enables investment in environmental management.

f.   The business leaders and the environmentalists actually have quite a lot in common if:

     i.   The business leaders can agree that their economic model needs to have a long-term sustainability focus by not depleting natural resources (and hence satisfying the environmentalists).

     ii.   The environmentalists can agree that businesses need to be sustainably viable from the short to the long term in order to generate economic Worth for all stakeholders and hence that some short-term compromises may be required (e.g. on the short-term mining of natural resources) to give businesses the cash-flow to shift to longer-term sustainable business practices (and hence satisfying the business leaders).

g.   So, it is entirely appropriate for subgroups to have different priorities and Worths and these might have different timescales, while acknowledging that in a multi-stakeholder environment some compromises may be necessary.

2.   Check that these relative Worths align with, or reasonably balance, the group's agreed overall Values and Fundamental Principles from Stage 1:

a.   The real-world Global and Motivational Worths generated in Stage 4 will probably have altered the stakeholder group's and subgroups' (possibly idealised) perceptions of overall Values and Fundamental Principles. It is essential that these Values and Fundamental Principles be reviewed and if necessary refined and agreed in this Stage 5 so that all investment decisions and their practical consequences contribute in various ways to generating the desired Worths.

b.   For example, as stakeholders in the CBD rejuvenation strategy worked through Stages 1 to 4 they will have become acutely aware of the interplay between economic, social, environmental and cultural factors. This may lead to an initial set of Values relating to financial viability (after all, this strategy is about a Central *Business* District) shifting to include more social, environmental and cultural parameters because sustainable businesses depend on sustainable social, environmental and cultural factors.

c.   It is likely that some Global Worths will be easy to agree on e.g. "businesses must be financially sustainable in the long term" while also agreeing that this does not mean that every business needs to be propped up to make it sustainable.

d.   Similarly, Fundamental Principles such as "we will not allow the water quality to be degraded" will probably be widely accepted by all stakeholders even if some stakeholders would prefer *all* water to not be degraded whereas others might be prepared to accept local degradation in return for water quality improvement in other locations.

3.   Check that each business case (*Validated SubStrategy*) is fully *Validated* in the context of the newly determined *relative Worths* including both Global Worth and Motivational Worths:

   a.   For the CBD rejuvenation strategy, the third Benefit ('feeling part of an integrated community') is likely to have been initially perceived by some stakeholders as a 'nice-to-have' but not essential. However, by Stage 5, this Benefit may now be viewed as essential and of high Worth in order to motivate the majority of stakeholders to spend more time in the CBD and hence enhance the financial sustainability of the businesses. In that scenario, the new magnitude of the Motivational Worth of this Benefit may mean that the SubStrategy needs to be tweaked in order that this Worth becomes widely perceived and does in fact motivate stakeholders to spend more time (and money) in the CBD.

4.   Prioritise investments in SubStrategies using the 3-step process recommended in *Validating Strategies*, pages 105–108.

   a.   Voting:

      i.   In this hypothetical example of the rejuvenation of a suburban CBD it is likely that most stakeholders will vote in favour of the first Project and its associated Results, Uses and Benefits because this Project is fundamental to the success of the CBD, both for the businesses and locals. So, both business and locals receive Motivational Benefits that are Worth-it.

   b.   Clustering of subgroups:

      i.   In contrast, support for the second Project is likely to be more mixed because it is not obvious that locals will receive any Motivational Benefits. Indeed, some locals may not want tourists and visitors to cause crowding and traffic congestion so may be actively opposed to this Project. So, a subgroup of tourism businesses may need to work hard to either convince a wider cross-section of stakeholders to support (or at least not

oppose) this Project. Maybe the tourism operators will offer to contribute to the environmental
Projects 5 and 6 in return for local support for
their Project 2.

ii.   Similarly environmental, education and recreational subgroups may combine to form a larger
subgroup which can contribute the resources to
run Projects 4 to 6 (environmental, recreational
and educational Projects).

c.   Clustering of SubStrategies:

i.   Projects 3 to 6 may individually not attract enough
support to enable them to go ahead. However, if
they can be merged and redesigned, then maybe
the   after-school-programmes   could   involve
environmental restoration Projects which simultaneously increase recreational opportunities.
For example, senior students could work with
a local polytechnic and environmental group to
build and maintain a boardwalk (with materials
supplied by a local company?) through a wetland adjacent to the CBD and to also establish
a student-run café overlooking the wetland and
backing on to the CBD.

5.   For major SubStrategies, probably undertake more comprehensive analyses using methods such as Better Business Case
or Investment Logic Mapping:

a.   The rejuvenation of a suburban CBD will require
many simultaneous actions to establish and drive
many complementary SubStrategies. So, even if each
SubStrategy has secured enough support for it to
be implemented, such implementation of individual SubStrategies may not be enough to achieve the
stakeholders' overall Benefits unless many of the key
Projects are implemented in the right sequence and in
a manner in which they complement each other.

b.   So for example, the businesses may not be prepared
to proceed with their agreed financially motivated
Projects 1 and 2 until they are certain that other groups
will definitely proceed with educationally, environmentally and recreationally motivated Projects 4 to 6

in a timely manner. The businesses will also almost certainly want a more detailed understanding of the magnitude of the impact on their businesses of these non-commercial projects and that will require the sort of a detailed socio-economic analysis that is done through BBC or ILM. Validated SubStrategies provide a robust basis for BBC/ILM analysis.

6.   Reconfirm the most relevant performance indicators and associated targets associated with each Project, Result, Use and Benefit so that they can be used to monitor the agreed priority Worths and Values:

a.   Check that the lead indicators will indeed indicate, at an early stage, whether the evolving strategy is working. For example, if the financial success of the CBD depends on increased numbers of wealthy tourists and visitors and if these customers will be attracted to the area primarily by the nearby environmental and recreational opportunities, then it may be necessary to add new lead indicators (e.g. bookings made through a tourism-marketing-website) to provide early indications about likely tourists and visitors:

    i.   numbers of tourists and visitors;
    ii.   types of accommodation and transport options booked;
    iii.   desired lengths of stays;
    iv.   types of recreational, educational, environmental and commercial opportunities booked;
    v.   whether or not they are likely to spend money in the CBD or just Use the free environmental and recreational opportunities.

b.   Also check if the lag indicators are still appropriate. For example, is the number of people visiting a beautiful environment adjacent to the CBD a useful indicator or would it be better to monitor the number of people who transition from the environment into the CBD *and* spend money?

c.   It may also be Worthwhile getting more detailed lag-information (on Benerfits) on what would motivate tourists and visitors to recommend the area to their friends and others so as to guide the development of more effective marketing strategies.

d.   It may also be worth monitoring whether or not tourists and visitors even know about the CBD's attractions (more of a lead indicator) because this indicator would also help guide the marketing strategies.

Accountabilities in Stage 5

Stage 5 accountabilities relate to finalising who will be accountable for each effectiveness and efficiency accountability, even if those accountabilities are subsequently subcontracted to other stakeholders in Stage 6: Create Performance-Based Contracts.

The issue of accountabilities in Stage 5 revolve primarily around a review and confirmation of the Global and Motivational Worths of those SubStrategies that have been selected for resourcing and implementing:

1.   The *nature* of the Benefits has already been determined in Stages 1–3 and the Global and Motivational *Worth* of Benefits of the full set of SubStrategies have already been determined in Stage 4.

2.   However, if in this Stage 5, it has been decided that not all SubStrategies will be implemented then the Global and Motivational Worths will now be different from at the end of Stage 4.

      a.   Some Benefits will no longer arise, so the Worth of those Benefits needs to be subtracted from the sum of the Worths used to calculate the net Global Worth of the overall set of SubStrategies and the Motivational Worths of each SubStrategy.

      b.   Similarly, the costs of the Projects and Uses associated with the un-supported SubStrategies also need to be subtracted from the costs used to determine the Global Worth and the Motivational Worths.

3.   Stage 5 will probably have altered the *relative* Worths of some SubStrategies to different stakeholder groups, so stakeholders need to be accountable in various ways for *reviewing and confirming* accountabilities of those SubStrategies that have been

selected for resourcing and implementing, i.e. reviewing and confirming:

a. Global Worth: Global Worth must still be positive in order to justify proceeding with the approved SubStrategies. The Global Worth of the approved SubStrategies must be demonstrably better than the Global Worth of the rejected SubStrategies. If all the SubStrategies have been well Validated and their Global and Motivational Worths well quantified, then it should be relatively straightforward to demonstrate which SubStrategies are *most* Worth-it.

b. Motivational Worth: Motivational Worth must still be sufficiently positive for each and every stakeholder to effectively motivate Uses to create Benefits, even in the absence of the rejected SubStrategies.

c. Project costs: Quantify Projects Efficiency for the approved Projects.

d. Use costs: Quantify Uses Efficiency for the approved Uses.

e. Indicators and targets: Stage 5 will probably have selected different indicators and targets from those selected in earlier stages in order to reflect the *relative* Worths of both Global and Motivational Benefits.

4. Responsibilities for reviewing and updating accountabilities for the approved SubStrategies (see also Chapter 3 for a table showing these responsibilities and accountabilities):

a. Quantifying the Global Worth of the full suite of approved SubStrategies is *primarily* the responsibility of all the purchasers collectively but will necessarily depend heavily on obtaining accurately quantified information from users on the Worth of the remaining Benefits to them and to others.

b. Quantifying the Motivational Worth of individual approved SubStrategies is *primarily* the responsibility of those purchasers who are investing in these SubStrategies but will necessarily depend heavily on obtaining accurately quantified information from all stakeholders on the Motivational Worth of the Benefits to them.

c. Quantifying Project Efficiency is *primarily* the responsibility of the suppliers of each Project.

d.   Quantifying the Use Efficiency with which Uses cre-
         ated Global Worth is *primarily* the responsibility of *all*
         purchasers collectively but will require accurately quan-
         titative information from end-users.

e.   Quantifying the Use Efficiency with which Uses cre-
         ate Motivational Worth is *primarily* the responsibil-
         ity of *purchasers of individual SubStrategies* but will
         require accurately quantitative information from
         end-users.

Comments

Recapping:

1.   The PRUB-Logic approach enables and encourages subgroups
         to operate independently yet collaboratively in such a man-
         ner that both the Global and Motivational Worths are positive.
         Most importantly, it means that each subgroup retains own-
         ership, responsibility, accountability and motivation for their
         own decisions and budgets by joining up budgets, not pooling
         budgets.

2.   Invariably there are more possible SubStrategies than there
         are funds and resources to enable them to happen.

3.   Even when a shorter list of *Validated* SubStrategies has been
         distilled there are usually still not enough resources and
         funds to fund them all.

4.   So, SubStrategies need to be compared to determine those that
         are *most* Worthwhile.

5.   But for whom are they *most* Worthwhile?

6.   Usually, there will be a number of SubStrategies that are seen
         as Worthwhile by all stakeholders, so these can be selected for
         implementation.

7.   Often, it is the case that some SubStrategies are high prior-
         ity for a subgroup, even if they are not a high priority for all
         stakeholders.

8.   So, a consequence can be that a number of subgroups fund
         and resource their priority SubStrategies quite independently
         of other SubStrategies while at the same time being fully
         aware of all other SubStrategies that are being implemented

and taking collaborative and complementary actions where appropriate.

9.   So, the OpenStrategies approach is quite different from the situation where all stakeholders pool their resources and collectively prioritise a master-list of business-cases/SubStrategies. That historical approach typically ends up supporting the *least controversial* business cases and fails to support business cases that are *high priority to subgroups*. It also leaves subgroups with no direct control of their decisions, budgets and motivations (because they have been handed over to the overall group of stakeholders) and this results in a lack of accountability that is seldom acceptable to the subgroups (especially to their financial controllers).

10.   The OpenStrategies PRUB-Logic approach: *"joins-up budgets rather than pools budgets"*.

Once your stakeholder groups have decided which SubStrategies to support and implement, then you are ready to move to Stage 6 – Create performance-based contracts (Chapter 9).

Chapter 9

Stage 6 – Create performance-based contracts

Reminder: Our purpose is *to enable and motivate Uses to create Benefits*

PRUB Mantra #1: *Only Uses create Benefits*

PRUB Mantra #2: Uses need the *right* Results or they won't happen

PRUB Mantra #3: Projects, Results, Uses and Benefits must be Linked with compelling Evidence

PRUB Mantra #4: SubStrategies must be Globally and Motivationally Worth it

PRUB Mantra #5: Invest in the 'best' SubStrategies

PRUB Mantra #6: Contracts define who does what for what rewards and Benefits

What is Stage 6?

Stage 6 will lock down the details of SubStrategies to enable effective and efficient implementation and accountability.

Stage 6 consists of agreeing and documenting exactly:

1.   who will do what, when, where, why, and how;
2.   the ways that these will be performance-managed;
3.   how contributors will be rewarded;
4.   legal factors.

What Stage 6 will achieve in order to support the other 8 stages

Stage 6 will produce crystal-clear contracts which includes:

1. All elements of the business case (the SubStrategy; the cause-and-effect Evidence; the Global and Motivational Worths).
2. Clear identification of the Effectiveness and Efficiency Accountabilities (PRUB-Accountabilities) in terms of performance management, i.e.:
    a. what indicators will be monitored including identifying and distinguishing lead and lag indicators;
    b. what the target values or Worths are for each indicator;
    c. what actions will be taken if targets are being missed;
    d. who is responsible for each category of accountability.
3. Traditional legal elements of contracts such as confidentiality, relevant laws, the country of jurisdiction, variations' procedures, dispute resolution procedures, contact details and so on. However, where 'suppliers' are in-house or otherwise closely associated with the purchasers, less formal contracts may suffice (see Figure 9.1).

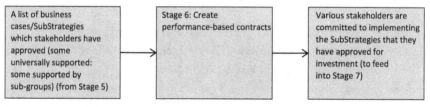

| A list of business cases/SubStrategies which stakeholders have approved (some universally supported: some supported by sub-groups) (from Stage 5) | Stage 6: Create performance-based contracts | Various stakeholders are committed to implementing the SubStrategies that they have approved for investment (to feed into Stage 7) |

Figure 9.1   The precursor to Stage 6, Stage 6 itself and what Stage 6 must feed into Stage 7.

WHY IS STAGE 6 IMPORTANT?

1. Contracts are the most important 'accountability documents' because they pin down what all parties agree on, and commit to, that is:
   a. what must actually be done;
   b. what will be achieved;
   c. when it will happen;
   d. who will do it;
   e. how progress will be monitored;
   f. how success will be measured;
   g. who will pay for it or resource it;
   h. who will Benefit from it;
   i. how changes can be proposed, agreed and made;
   j. legal parameters.
2. Once all parties agree to the contract, expectations are aligned and everyone knows what their role is and what their recompense will be.
3. So, an effective contract will be crystal clear on all accountabilities so that no-one is in any doubt about who is responsible for what and so that account-abilities cannot be retrospectively changed unless all parties agree to modify the contract.
4. Purchasers will be clear on what they will 'get' for their investment.
5. Suppliers will be clear on what they must create, how they will be measured, what their targets are and what they will be paid for their contributions.
6. Beneficiaries will be clear on what they will 'get' (Results) that they can Use to create Benefits.
7. Subsequent renegotiations or contract disputes will be simplified because there will be clear reference points in the initial agreement to guide any arguments.

Summary of the start-to-finish action sequence for Stage 6

Stages 1 to 5 have created well-*Validated* SubStrategies with clearly defined accountabilities and approved the best ones to invest in and implement.

It should now be straightforward to formalise those SubStrategies into contract documents, probably with input from legal experts.

1. The PRUB-related components are:

    a. import into the contract the *Validated* SubStrategies and accountabilities that were approved for investment in Stage 5;

    b. if necessary, develop *Sub*-SubStrategies that define more detailed contractual steps especially in relation to Projects and their milestones;

    c. distribute the elements of the sub-SubStrategies appropriately between contracts with different suppliers while ensuring that these contracts complement each other in an integrated way.

2. The non-PRUB-related components are:

    a. incorporate the *Validated* SubStrategies and accountabilities within legally robust contracts.

Explanation of the start-to-finish action sequence for Stage 6

1. The PRUB-related components are:

    a. Import into the contracts the *Validated* SubStrategies and accountabilities from Stage 5:

        i. In this Stage 6, all the elements of the SubStrategies, performance management criteria and accountabilities identified and quantified in earlier stages now get *contractually specified*.

        ii. Stages 1 to 5 produced *Validated* SubStrategies together with performance indicators, targets and defined accountabilities and these can simply be imported into contracts between purchasers and suppliers.

        iii. It is recommended that contracts include all levels of SubStrategies, with the high-level Aspirational SubStrategy defining the overarching intentions and context for the supporting Guidance-level SubStrategies.

iv.   In large-scale multi-stakeholder strategies, it is likely that a number of different purchasers and suppliers will be involved, so a number of contracts will be required. If the overall OpenStrategy is to be implemented effectively and efficiently, then this means that the contracting and implementation of sub-SubStrategies needs to be integrated across purchasers and suppliers. This integration is made *as simple as possible* by using the common language of PRUB-Logic-based SubStrategies.

b.   If necessary, develop sub-SubStrategies that define more detailed contractual steps especially in relation to Projects and their milestones:

i.   SubStrategies that have been developed as business cases (Stage 4) and used for decision making (Stage 5) may not contain sufficient day-to-day detail for contractual purposes, especially for subcontracts.

ii.   Stage 6 is therefore likely to involve creating *sub*-SubStrategies which provide more detail, especially about Projects and their milestones. Alternatively, the contracts developed in this stage may specify that more detailed sub-SubStrategies, indicators and targets be created as the *first part of the implementation process* (Stage 7).

iii.   Either way, such sub-SubStrategies should be created in the same PRUB-Logic format as the SubStrategies that emerged from Stages 1 to 5 so that it is easy for stakeholders to align and correlate the different levels of SubStrategies.

2. The non-PRUB-related components are:

a.   Incorporate the *Validated* SubStrategies and accountabilities within legally robust contracts:

i.   It is recommended that readers seek professional legal advice on drafting the contract which incorporates the SubStrategies, their performance management parameters and accountabilities because what will be required will vary enormously depending on the size of the contracts and the country of jurisdiction.

ii.   The key point here is that Stages 1 to 5 have generated the core ingredients of contracts so it should be straightforward for a legal expert to insert these into effective and legally binding contract.

Demonstration of Stage 6 actions

The incomplete, high-level Childhood Obesity SubStrategy introduced in Stage 2 Chapter 5 is repeated in Figure 9.2.

In practice, in Stages 1 to 4, this SubStrategy would have been expanded to also include high-level Projects and Results to enable the first and second Uses (Children exercising more; children eating more healthily).

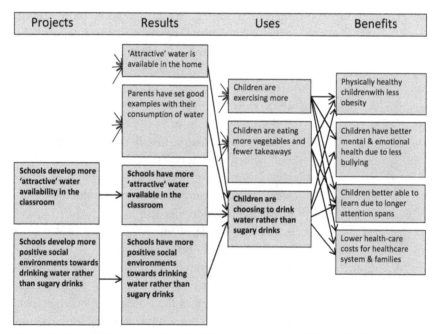

Figure 9.2   The emerging SubStrategy on childhood obesity from Stage 2, Chapter 5.

So, this strategy would now contain three main SubStrategies to enable and motivate the three desired Uses. However, for contractual purposes it may be most effective to have:

a.   three multi-supplier contracts: one associated with each Use; or

b.   four single-contracts: one associated with each of the four Results; or

c.   two single-supplier contracts:

   i.   one 'contract' with parents to encourage them to commit to providing healthy food and water at home and in children's lunches that they consume at school; and

   ii.   one 'contract' with schools so that they develop more attractive water in schools and a more positive social environment towards drinking water.

There is no 'right' combination of contracts as any one of the above three options could be made to work and each option has advantages and disadvantages. For example:

a.   The three multi-supplier, Use-oriented contracts would have the advantages that:

   i.   their focus is strongly on enabling and motivating Uses;

   ii.   they would require suppliers to work collaboratively and so, ideally, create well-integrated Results that would actually be Used effectively.

   These same three multi-supplier contracts would have the disadvantage that:

   iii.   they would require suppliers to work collaboratively, so while this may be ideal in terms of integrating Results, it can be difficult practically and contractually if the different suppliers have different modes of working and different levels of commitment to effective performance.

b.   The four single-supplier contracts would have the advantage that:

   i.   each supplier could work independently without needing to collaborate with other suppliers.

The four single-supplier, Results-oriented contracts would have the disadvantages that:

ii. The focus would be on Results rather than Uses. This may be no problem if the Results definitely are the right and best Results and will definitely be Used to create Benefits. However, the Results-based contracts risk suppliers losing their focus on the *effectiveness* of the full set of Results that they must create to enable and motivate Uses to create Benefits.

iii. The four separate contracts may struggle to fully *integrate* their Results to best-enable and motivate Uses to create Benefits.

c. Two single-supplier contracts

i. A 'contract' with parents would necessarily be rather different from a contract with a commercial supplier. In the above example, it is likely that the *Validated* SubStrategy would have had input from a fairly small group of parents who would readily buy-in to the idea of committing to a programme of healthy eating, drinking and exercise for their children. However, for the programme to achieve widespread success it would be necessary to bring many more parents on-board. This would probably lead to recognition of a need for another SubStrategy along the lines of: "Promote and secure the commitment of most parents to guide and enable their children to eat, drink and exercise in healthy ways" with a suite of Projects to motivate parents.

So, this is an example of a supplier (parents) being a 'voluntary supplier' who cannot be forced, or motivated by payment, to make their contributions to the SubStrategy, yet their role is crucial to the success of the SubStrategy. To secure parental support, it will be necessary to convince parents that there are sufficient Benefits to them and/or their children to motivate the parents to contribute. This once again highlights the importance of understanding *Motivational Worth* to each and every stakeholder whose contributions to the SubStrategy are essential for it to achieve its desired Benefits.

    ii.   A 'contract' with a school would probably be simpler, encouraging the school to make water drinking more attractive and socially desirable.

Accountabilities in Stage 6

1.   This stage *contractually specifies* the intended Effectiveness and Efficiency Accountabilities.

2.   This specification stage is *jointly* the responsibility of purchasers and suppliers because it requires negotiation to agree on:
    a.   who is ultimately accountable for ensuring actual Project Efficiency; Result Effectiveness; Use Efficiency; and Benefit Effectiveness;
    b.   if and how some of these accountabilities will be sub-contracted to other stakeholders.

3.   Too often, suppliers are (sometimes retrospectively) 'held accountable' by purchasers for all aspects of accountability (*both* effectiveness and efficiency) even though the suppliers had no control over Results Effectiveness, Benefits Effectiveness or Use Efficiency because it was the purchaser who decided what services, products and infrastructure to purchase.

4.   By separating Effectiveness Accountability for Results and Benefits from Efficiency Accountability for Projects and Uses, it is possible to separate the ownership of these accountabilities, respectively:
    a.   purchasers are accountable for both Results Effectiveness and Benefits Effectiveness;
    b.   suppliers are accountable for Projects Efficiency;
    c.   purchasers are accountable for Uses Efficiency.

5.   Invariably there will be some overlaps in the types of accountabilities and who is responsible for them.

6.   However, it is still essential at the contract writing stage to delineate all 4 PRUB-Accountabilities, and the responsibilities for these PRUB-Accountabilities, as much as it is possible to do, so that all stakeholders are crystal clear on what they must achieve.

7.   In particular, it needs to be reaffirmed that the purchaser remains ultimately accountable for having correctly identified and quantified both Results Effectiveness and Benefits

Effectiveness because *they are the entity that is deciding what are the right things to do.*

Comments

1.   Contracts are the most important documents in the 9-stage OpenStrategies-process because they specify exactly who will apply which resources to *create Results that will enable and motivate Uses to create Benefits.*

2.   The preparation of contracts will be straightforward if Stages 1 to 5 have created robustly *Validated* SubStrategies together with well-defined performance management parameters and associated accountabilities.

3.   A contract with this content will, when implemented, enable and motivate Uses to create Benefits.

4.   In our experience, contracts tend to be at the level of Guidance-level Strategies. Therefore, they are more detailed than high-level Aspirational strategies but not as detailed as grassroots-level Operational strategies.

5.   So, Stage 6 reaps the benefits of the necessary and sufficient hard work that was done in Stages 1–5.

6.   If Stages 1 to 5 have not been completed rigorously then it will be almost impossible to create a fair and effective contract, or set of contracts, that when implemented will *definitely enable and motivate Uses to create Benefits.* (If you, as reader, disagree, please email us telling us which elements of Stages 1 to 5 are not necessary – or which elements are missing – for underpinning an effective contract: phil@openstrategies.com).

Once you have effective contracts in place you are ready to move to Stage 7 – Implementing Validated Strategies.

Chapter 10

Stage 7 – Implement strategies

Reminder: Our purpose is *to enable and motivate Uses to create Benefits*

PRUB Mantra #1: *Only Uses create Benefits*

PRUB Mantra #2: Uses need the *right* Results or they won't happen

PRUB Mantra #3: Projects, Results, Uses and Benefits must be Linked with compelling Evidence

PRUB Mantra #4: SubStrategies must be Globally and Motivationally Worth it

PRUB Mantra #5: Invest in the 'best' SubStrategies

PRUB Mantra #6: Contracts define who does what for what rewards and Benefits

PRUB Mantra #7: Implement with confidence

What is Stage 7?

In Stage 7, stakeholders do the right things in the right ways that *'enable and motivate Uses to create Benefits'* – *with confidence* that their approved suite of Validated SubStrategies will be effective and efficient.

Stage 7 typically consists of (many) stakeholders running (many) Projects to produce (many) Results that enable and motivate (many) Uses to create (many) Benefits which have both Global plus Motivational Worths for each and every stakeholder who needs to contribute to the success of the strategy implementation.

What Stage 7 will achieve in order to support the other 8 stages

Stage 7 will:

1. *Create Results that enable and motivate Uses to create Benefits.*
2. Create information that can be used (in parallel or in sequence in Stage 8) to performance-manage this implementation, and in Stage 9 to update the SubStrategies (see Figure 10.1).

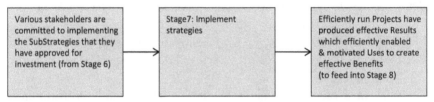

Figure 10.1   The precursor to Stage 7, Stage 7 itself and what Stage 7 must feed into Stage 8.

WHY IS STAGE 7 IMPORTANT?

1. The whole point of the 9-stage OpenStrategies process is to get stuff done to *enable and motivate Uses to create Benefits* – i.e: to implement strategies.
2. The other 8 stages improve the way a strategy is developed and how implementation is managed, so they are important, but if implementation doesn't happen then the other 8 stages are a total waste of time.

Summary of the start-to-finish action sequence for Stage 7

1. Develop operational-level project management plans based on the contractually defined SubStrategies with their performance management and accountability criteria from Stage 6.
2. Interlink these SubStrategies so that their implementation is complementary.
3. *Manage* Projects efficiently to create effective Results.

4.   *Influence* Uses to efficiently create effective Benefits.

5.   Generate information that can be used in Stage 8 to improve performance and in Stage 9 to review the overall performance of the strategy.

Explanation of the start-to-finish action sequence for Stage 7

1.   Develop operational-level project management plans based on the contractually defined SubStrategies with their performance management and accountability criteria from Stage 6:

   a.   Strategies and contracts are generally written at an Aspirational or Guidance level (see *Validating Strategies*, pages 14–16) which do not provide enough detail for day-to-day project management. However, the contractual PRUB-Logic-based SubStrategies do provide strong guidance, especially in relation to Uses and Benefits and hence the necessary and sufficient Results required to enable and motivate those Benefits.

   b.   Frequently, the first thing to do in this stage of implementation is to create more detailed Operational-level SubStrategies which will define specific actions consistent with the very high-level Aspirational SubStrategies that are guiding the entire 9-stage process and with the Guidance-level SubStrategies that are part of the contract document from Stage 6.

   c.   These Operational-level SubStrategies take key Projects from the Guidance-level SubStrategies and disaggregate them into their component parts, also in the form of SubStrategies. Often the Uses and Benefits stay the same as in the Guidance-level SubStrategies with the Projects and Results being disaggregated into more detailed steps.

   d.   More detail is most often required within Projects, i.e. exactly: what will be done; by whom; by when; what is the critical path; how will resources be distributed and so on.

   e.   Because these details are part of normal, widely adopted project management activities it is unnecessary to describe them here. Organisations such as the Project Management Institute (https://www.pmi.org/) or the Association of Project Managers (https://www.apm.org.uk/) have a wealth of information on project management tools and methodologies for running projects, programmes and portfolios.

2.   Interlink these SubStrategies so that their implementation is complementary:

a.   In multi-stakeholder situations in which many different organisations and individuals will be implementing numerous SubStrategies, it is particularly important to develop, share and interlink Operational-level SubStrategies. This helps ensure that each stakeholder knows what the others are doing and can interlink their actions. This will help avoid duplication, mitigate adverse effects and encourage multiple possible Uses. For example, in a 'recreation and fitness' strategy plus a separate 'exercise' SubStrategies for older people and for children, it would make sense to at least consider linking these SubStrategies, perhaps to share resources or even to exercise together.

3.   *Manage* Projects to efficiently create effective Results.

Individual organisations can draw on a wealth of information on project, programme and portfolio management as noted earlier, so these topics will not be discussed here. These normal project management methods can guide the running of Projects so that they produce the right Results on-time and within budget. If the preceding 6 stages have been completed thoroughly, then there will be a high level of confidence that these Results will be both necessary and sufficient to effectively and efficiently *enable and motivate Uses to create Benefits.*

Projects need to be run collaboratively or at least with an awareness of other Projects. This is where SubStrategies really come into their own because:

a.   They succinctly describe each and every action in ways that all stakeholders can understand.

b.   They are easy to interconnect across organisations, across themes and across end-users because they use the same simple PRUB-Logic information structure and this simplifies collaboration.

c.   They include both Global and Motivational Worths and as such define the 'big picture' reasons why the strategies need to be implemented (Global Worth) as well as defining the 'what's in it for me' Motivational Worth for each and every stakeholder.

d.   Project managers can control/manage their Projects to ensure they produce the required Results.

4.   *Influence* Uses to efficiently create effective Benefits:

a.   Uses are almost always voluntary, so *users cannot be compelled to undertake Uses.* SubStrategies that were approved for investment and were contractually specified in Stage 6 will ideally have recognised this and will have included Projects which inform, train and motivate users to undertake the Uses to create Benefits with sufficient Global and Motivational Worths.

b.   This step of *influencing* Uses to create Benefits will consist of implementing such informational Projects that create Results that inform, train (where necessary), facilitate access to Results and motivate users to undertake the Uses.

c.   'Influencing' is not easy. It requires an in-depth understanding of end-users' motivations for undertaking the Uses and making sure that the *right* set of *necessary and sufficient Results* are provided so that these motivations (Benefits) actually emerge from the Uses as intended. It may transpire that the intended Benefits/Motivations are not enough to motivate the Uses so implementation may need to change to create *sufficient* motivations.

5.   Generate information that can be used in Stage 8 to monitor and improve performance and in Stage 9 to review the overall performance of the strategy (refer also to Chapter 3 on Accountabilities):

a.   Implementation and performance management are intimately interlinked, with implementation making stuff happen and performance management monitoring and then influencing the quality, quantity and timing of what is being done and achieved.

b.   Because the greatest uncertainty relating to performance frequently relates to whether or not Uses really will happen and will create Benefits as intended, monitoring and where necessary improving the users' experiences is crucial.

c.   Assuming Stages 1 to 5 have correctly identified the *right* Results to *enable and motivate Uses to create Benefits,* then collecting information on the *progress* of the Projects and the *quality* of the Results should enable performance management (Stage 8) to predict whether or not the desired Uses and Benefits are likely to actually happen.

d.   However, in this complex world it is likely that some Results will not be used or will be used differently from what was predicted from the earlier stages, so this situation needs to be detected as soon as possible and the SubStrategies (and contracts) modified where necessary.

e.   In complex situations with many SubStrategies being implemented in parallel, it is also essential to collect performance monitoring information on how different SubStrategies impact on each other.

f.   It will be near impossible for any single stakeholder to check that all the right performance monitoring information is being collected across all SubStrategies. It is therefore both an individual and collective responsibility to identify what information needs to be collected within each SubStrategy (as contractually specified) and across SubStrategies (which may not have been contractually specified). This needs to be done by the people who are implementing and/or funding each individual SubStrategy by constantly scanning the environment to check what other SubStrategies are being implemented and then engaging with the project managers for those SubStrategies to identify and monitor cross-SubStrategy implementation.

g.   It is necessary to monitor Projects and Results (lead indicators) for guiding performance management in Stage 8 and to monitor Uses and Benefits (lag indicators) for guiding re-optimisations (if necessary) of the overall strategy (Stage 9).

h.   Performance monitoring information is frequently used to justify payments to suppliers based on the extent to which they have developed the products, services and infrastructure they have been contracted to produce.

i. It is therefore essential that those stakeholders who are implementing and/or funding SubStrategies actively monitor and respond to the contractually specified performance indicators so that, where agreed, they can provide performance monitoring data to other key stakeholders so that they get appropriately recompensed for what they have created.

Demonstration of Stage 7 actions

How would this work in the example of a large-scale, multi-stakeholder situation such as the redevelopment of a central business district (CBD)?

1. Develop operational-level project management plans based on the contractually defined (from Stage 6) SubStrategies with their performance management and accountability criteria.

This example from Stages 1 and 5 included the 2 Projects and Results shown in Figure 10.2.

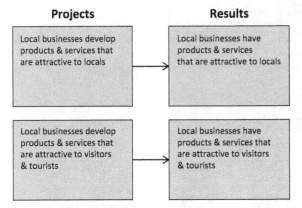

Figure 10.2   Two Projects and Results distilled from the SubStrategy to redevelop a central business district.

These 2 Projects are too high-level to be implemented.

They also involve many different stakeholders (many businesses; many users with different interests) who ideally need to work together to provide integrated packages of products and services that maximise the Uses and Benefits.

So, at this implementation Stage 7, it is essential to develop a suite of more detailed, interlinked sub-SubStrategies which are guided by the contractually approved Guidance-level SubStrategies from Stage 6.

In this example, it is likely to be appropriate to start by getting stakeholders (businesses; local government; NGOs and others) to collaboratively develop operational-level sub-SubStrategies that help guide their individual actions so that when implemented collaboratively they achieve more than what would be achieved if each action was taken in isolation. This is shown in Figure 10.3, which outlines *some* of the

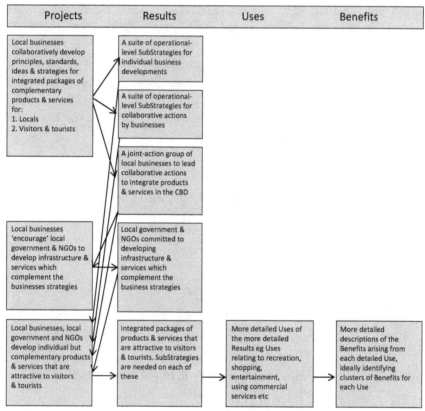

Figure 10.3   Some initial operational-level 'Projects/Results' for guiding the integration of multiple products and services so that they are optimised for locals, tourists and visitors. Only the final Result is actually 'Useful' by end-users – all the others are 'Adoptable Orphan Results'.

operational-level planning steps that would ideally be taken. Even more detailed sub-Sub-SubStrategies would emerge from this SubStrategy as identified in the first two Results.

The first Project includes the development of principles and standards for the CBD redevelopment, the details of which will address such issues as:

- The general themes for the area, e.g. including:
  - open and spacious?
  - focus on efficiency?
  - focus on interconnectedness with the community?
  - holiday or business atmosphere?
  - clean-green/sustainable?
- The main types of Uses and Results:
  - primarily offices and cafes?
  - primarily retail?
  - primarily recreation and entertainment facilities?
  - significant permanent accommodation or will local accommodation be encouraged just outside the CBD?
  - significant tourist accommodation and where this will be best located?
- How the different Uses will be optimised by interlinking:
  - how accommodation suppliers will encourage visitors and tourists to use the local products and services;
  - how businesses will feed customers to each other.

Many of these more detailed sub-SubStrategies will require revisiting the information collected in Stages 1 to 6 in order to gain detailed clarity, especially in relation to Uses. In this example, it will be essential to fully comprehend the Uses by visitors and tourists so as to guide the development of the *best* infrastructure, *best* products and *best* services to optimise the Global and Motivational Worths of the overall regeneration strategy.

Note that in the SubStrategy in Figure 10.3, the first 4 Results will not be directly Used by locals, tourists and visitors but instead will be Adopted by other Projects (see *Validating Strategies,* pages 44–46). The first few Projects and Results are still essential because together they enable the 5th Result that in turn will *enable and motivate Uses to create Benefits.*

2.   Interlink these SubStrategies so that their implementation is complementary:

Because in complex situations like the regeneration of a CBD almost no actions take place in isolation, it is imperative that SubStrategies be interlinked wherever it is appropriate and possible. This will minimise duplication, enhance the complementarity of SubStrategies and help keep different SubStrategies aligned with each other. So, instead of running individual Projects and their associated SubStrategies, it is essential to simultaneously run 'portfolios of linked SubStrategies'. This is why in the mock-up SubStrategy shown in Figure 10.3 the third Result identifies a joint action group to coordinate the interlinking of SubStrategies.

In order to optimise the Global and Motivational Worths to all stakeholders, many of the desired Uses need to be integrated so as to influence those Uses to create the optimum Benefits. So for example, the nature of the redeveloped streetscapes needs to align with their Uses for:

- entertainment and recreation (e.g. the integrated Uses of cafes; street markets; places to meet and sit in the sun; theatres; perhaps a sense of 'vibrancy');
- commerce (e.g. the integrated Uses of parking; access to professional services; retail; perhaps a sense of 'efficiency' or 'profitability');
- environmental well-being (e.g. the integrated effects on Uses of air quality; noise minimisation; natural habitats; wind speeds; shelter from rain; perhaps a sense of 'healthiness').

SubStrategies based on PRUB-Logic can readily be blended and restructured to help guide this integration.

3.   *Manage* Projects in well-controlled ways to create Results:

Given the huge amount of literature and training programmes on project management, this does not need to be discussed here.

4.   *Influence* Uses to create Benefits:

By now the reader may be tired of reading that 'Uses can only be *influenced*'. But if strategies are going to be effective, it is essential that not only does the reader 'get-it' but also that *all* stakeholders also 'get-it' – that Uses can only be *influenced* to create Benefits. In our extensive experience with many multi-stakeholder groups and thousands of stakeholders we find that many stakeholders, especially stakeholders in organisations, cling to the belief that Uses can be *managed*. This belief leads to a number of problems, including:

a.   purchasers believing that 'obviously and surely the Uses will happen' because the Uses are the sorts of Uses that the purchasers themselves might use, even if they are not the sorts of Uses that the actual end-users will Use;

b.   purchasers wrongly blaming suppliers for failing to 'manage' Uses or to 'make Uses happen' or for Uses to create Benefits (outcomes) when it is often the case that the purchasers purchased the wrong Projects/Results which therefore were not, voluntarily, Used as hoped.

So, in the example of the redevelopment of a CBD:

a.   *Influencing* a Use such as 'people are shopping for weekly supplies' could include:

i.   marketing the retail sector to target customers;

ii.   providing appropriate transport for the target customers;

iii.   providing such good customer experiences that customer tell others;

iv.   running 'buy-local' campaigns;

v.   providing complementary services so that shopping becomes part of a larger CBD experience;

vi.   having appropriate access provisions for all users;

vii.   having adequate opening hours to accommodate full-time workers;

viii.   stocking locally preferred products;

ix.   offering competitively priced goods and services.

b.   *Influencing* a Use such as 'people are cycling recreationally' could include:

x.   providing bikes-to-hire (with user-friendly pay-
        ment options) together with helmets and other
        safety equipment;

xi.   providing well-signposted cycling trails with
        different levels of difficulty;

xii.   providing trail maps that clip to the handlebars
        of bikes;

xiii.   having cafes and shelters conveniently located
        on or near the trails;

xiv.   having brochures and signboards that identify
        interesting features along the trails;

xv.   providing training courses in off-road recrea-
        tional cycling;

xvi.   providing secure lock-up facilities for bicycles;

xvii.   providing public showers (for cyclists) in the
        CBD or subsidised in a local gymnasium.

These examples demonstrate the importance of having
explicit information on Uses because this Uses-information
strongly guides what is required in terms of Results. When
we developed PRUB-Logic we initially believed that strategies
needed to be guided primarily by Benefits but we soon discov-
ered that the most compellingly useful information is 'Uses'.

Certainly, it is important to know what the Benefits will
be so that investors in a SubStrategy know what will ultimately emerge from the implementation of the SubStrategies.
However, the Benefits on their own provide very little guidance as to what Results will enable and motivate the Uses.

This reconfirms why Stage 1 in the 9-stage process is
critically important because it identifies and precisely defines
desired actual Uses (which tend to be situation-specific) and
Benefits (which tend to be more generic).

5.   Generate information that can be used in Stage 8 to monitor
      and improve performance and in Stage 9 to review the effec-
      tiveness of the overall strategy:

      a.   in the complex world of the redevelopment of a CBD
            it will be necessary to collect performance monitor-
            ing information on each SubStrategy, as contractually
            specified, and also on how the different SubStrategies
            are complementing or impeding each other.

b.   So, for example, information needs to be collected to confirm that:

   i.   The transport SubStrategy for enabling people to get to the CBD for shopping and using commercial services is also working for people who want to visit the CBD as part of a recreational cycling experience, or at least not impeding them.

   ii.   The SubStrategy for creating a convivial urban streetscape is being implemented in a way that still enables trucks to deliver goods to local businesses.

   iii.   The SubStrategy for promoting free recreational activities is aligned with the retail strategy for attracting recreationalists into the CBD for shopping and entertainment.

c.   The above small set of examples confirm that it will be near impossible for any single stakeholder to check that all the right performance monitoring information is being collected. This is further confirmation of why strategies need to be understood by large numbers of stakeholders – so they can be implemented and performance managed by many of these same stakeholders with oversight by the purchasers/funders of the suite of SubStrategies. As our OpenStrategies by-line says, this requires 'liberating collective wisdom' with an emphasis on 'liberating' not 'controlling/managing' collective wisdom.

Accountabilities in Stage 7

During implementation:

1.   Suppliers are accountable for delivering on their promises of efficiently creating the Results that were specified in Stage 6 (contracts).

2.   If suppliers are efficiently creating the Results that the purchasers have contracted them to create, then the suppliers cannot reasonably be held accountable for the effectiveness

of how those Results are Used to create Benefits because the Links from Results to Uses and from Uses to Benefits are the responsibility of purchasers.

3.   As the Results become available it will become increasingly clear whether or not Uses are happening and generating Benefits. At this point, purchasers will find out if they made good decisions on Effectiveness-accountability (i.e. did they invest in the best business cases/SubStrategies?).

Comments

1.   The purpose of all 9 stages is to effectively and efficiently enable 'Stage 7: implementation' – i.e. to actually make things happen.

2.   Stages 1–6 and 8 and 9 are 'talk and paperwork'. They do not actually make real-world things happen although they are nevertheless essential for guiding the *right* things to happen (effectiveness) *in the right way* (efficiency).

3.   While the above two statements appear obvious, far too often a lot of effort is put into Stages 1–4 (end-user engagement; supplier engagement; strategising; creating business cases) at which point the process stops because no-one is prepared to commit to making binding decisions that may require new resources or require the reallocation of resources from exist-ing activities. This is an unfortunate reality in this world. However, by having all competing ideas represented in the same format as succinct, convincingly *Validated* SubStrategies and business cases, it makes it easier for stakeholders to make decisions and convince their constituents that the implemen-tation decisions are good ones.

4.   The first half of implementing *Validated* SubStrategies – Projects creating Results – is generally straightforward because this first half of the PRUB sequence is usually under the *control/ management* of a small number of suppliers.

5.   The second half of implementing *Validated* SubStrategies – Uses creating Benefits – is more challenging because pur-chasers, suppliers and others can only *influence* the Uses and Benefits – they cannot *control/manage* them. The stronger the

Validation of the SubStrategy, the stronger this influence will be on the Uses and Benefits – but it cannot be guaranteed.

Stage 7, Implementation, needs to be accompanied by effective performance management as will now be described in Stage 8, Performance-Manage strategies (Chapter 11).

Chapter 11

Stage 8 – Performance-manage strategies

Reminder: Our purpose is *to enable and motivate Uses to create Benefits*

PRUB Mantra #1: *Only Uses create Benefits*

PRUB Mantra #2: Uses need to have the *right* Results or they won't happen

PRUB Mantra #3: Projects, Results, Uses and Benefits must be Linked with compelling Evidence

PRUB Mantra #4: SubStrategies must be Globally and Motivationally Worth it

PRUB Mantra #5: Invest in the 'best' SubStrategies

PRUB Mantra #6: Contracts define who does what for what rewards and Benefits

PRUB Mantra #7: Implement with confidence

PRUB Mantra #8: You do not fatten the pig by measuring it. You must take action on performance measurements

What is Stage 8?

Stage 8 consists of monitoring the implementation of *current* Projects, Results, Uses and Benefits to check that they are evolving as contracted. If not, then Stage 8 improves the Projects to more efficiently produce more useable Results which better *enable and motivate Uses to create Benefits*. So, Stage 8 focuses on improving *efficiency* in the *current* strategy.

In contrast to this Stage 8, Stage 9 reviews the overall strategy itself to check if it is still the most *effective* strategy and updates it to make it more appropriate and effective or even replaces it with a better strategy. Stages 8 and 9 invariably overlap but for clarity they are discussed separately here.

So, Stage 8 focuses on *efficiency in the current strategy* (doing current things right) and Stage 9 focuses on *effectiveness of the current and future strategies* (doing the right things even if that means doing new things).

What Stage 8 will achieve in order to support the other 8 stages

1. Stage 8 *must* include performance *management* and not just monitoring ("You do not fatten the pig by measuring it").

2. Stage 8 will stimulate and guide the implementation (back in Stage 7) of new Project-actions being taken by suppliers and suppliers where this is necessary due to the implementation of the contracted SubStrategies turning out to be less *efficient* than expected. So, Stage 8 focuses on identifying *how the contracted SubStrategies are being implemented* and what needs changing to improve the *efficiency*, not on whether or not they are the best SubStrategies (that is done in Stage 9).

3. Stage 8 is also likely to identify where SubStrategies are turning out to be less *effective* than expected. This information will underpin robust decisions on making changes to the SubStrategies in Stage 9. To make such decisions it may be necessary to revisit Stages 1 to 7 in order to update the strategies, decisions, contracts and implementation to achieve the desired Benefits.

4. These decisions must be based on robust monitoring information of both lead and lag indicators (respectively: indicators/targets/measurements for Projects/Results and for Uses/Benefits). Lead indicators are measures of *progress* whereas lag indicators are measures of *success* (see Figure 11.1).

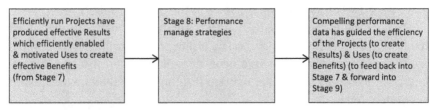

Figure 11.1   The precursor to Stage 8, Stage 8 itself and what Stage 8 must feed into Stage 9.

WHY IS STAGE 8 IMPORTANT?

1. Implementation of strategies needs to be constantly monitored and updated because the real world is so complex that the implementation of strategies seldom proceeds fully as expected, for example:

    a. Cause-and-effect Evidence that initially appeared robust may turn out to be incorrect due to factors that were not initially evident or considered relevant

    b. Conditions change over time so that SubStrategies that were fully *Validated* initially may no longer be *Validated*

    c. The implementation of SubStrategies can have unintended consequences both within each SubStrategy and also in the ways each SubStrategy impacts on other SubStrategies.

2. Lead indicators associated with Projects and Results give an early indication of whether or not the Projects are proceeding to produce the *right* Results (*effectiveness*) as *efficiently* as desired. So, lead indicators provide information that can be acted on early in the implementation process and will affect primarily Project-Efficiency and Result-Effectiveness (are the Projects efficiently producing effective Results?). Think of lead indicators as 'progress indicators'.

3. Lag indicators associated with Uses and Benefits provide later indications of whether or not the Results are actually being Used and whether or not the Uses are actually creating the desired Benefits. So, lag indicators provide information that can be acted on later in the implementation process and will affect primarily Use-Efficiency and Benefit-Effectiveness (are the Results being efficiently Used to create effective Benefits?) Think of lag indicators as 'success indicators'. Note however that some lag indicators such as 'customer complaints' (which arise through a Use) can feed back into the *next iteration* of a SubStrategy so can sometimes be confusingly thought of as lead indicators. They are simultaneously lag indicators of the first iteration of a SubStrategy and lead indicator inputs into the next iteration of the SubStrategy.

4. Information on lead and lag indicators therefore guides the implementation of existing SubStrategies (Stage 7) and, where necessary, the redesign of the overall suite of SubStrategies (Stage 9).

5. In all the above cases, simply monitoring lead and lag indicators is a waste of time and resources if no performance management action is taken.

Summary of the start-to-finish action sequence for Stage 8

1.   Determine if the contractually specified indicators, Evidence and targets are still relevant for monitoring and managing

individual SubStrategies *and* for monitoring and managing the interactions between SubStrategies, and agree on a final set of indicators and targets.

2.   Inform all stakeholders of the indicators, Evidence and targets for each Project, Result, Uses and Benefit and reconfirm with them why it is important to collect this information.

3.   Monitor the performance indicators and the cause-and-effect Evidence sufficiently often to underpin decision making to improve the performance of existing strategies in Stage 7 and to improve or create new strategies in Stage 9.

4.   Decision makers make wise, performance-enhancing decisions about existing SubStrategies based on reliable performance monitoring information and on cause-and-effect Evidence.

5.   Project teams implement the new, performance-enhancing decisions.

Explanation of the start-to-finish sequence for Stage 8

1.   Determine if the contractually specified indicators, Evidence and targets are still relevant for monitoring and managing individual SubStrategies *and* for monitoring and managing the interactions between SubStrategies and agree on a final set of indicators and targets:

a.   If contracts (Stage 6) have been well written based on earlier Stages 1–5, then there should be clear sets of indicators and Evidence that need monitoring and to be compared with targets in order to enable effective performance management and decision making. However, in large complex Projects, these indicators and Evidence are likely to be relatively high level because it would be impractical to include all of them in each and every contract.

b.   There is a well-known phrase: "if you cannot measure it then you cannot manage it". Sadly this often gets misinterpreted as: "if we are measuring it then we must be managing it". As a consequence, a huge amount of effort is expended in measuring just about everything that moves but almost nothing is done with the data. Do not fall into this trap! Measurement does not equate to management.

c.   It is therefore important to review the contractually specified indicators, Evidence and targets to check that they really are *practical and useful* for guiding actions at the level of day-to-day operations.

d.   Check that at the operational, day-to-day level that the selected indicators and Evidence can be monitored cost-effectively and will definitely produce information that will actually be used to continually improve performance. Collecting data can be time-consuming, expensive and irritating so *do not collect it unless you know you will act on it,*

e.   Check with people on the ground who are managing projects so as to make sure that the information that is collected will genuinely *help them* improve performance and is not just some set of data that 'someone somewhere' decided should be collected. 'More data' isn't always better. Always aim to obtain and use 'useful *indicators'* (Remember the OpenStrategies' dictum: *"the smallest amount of information that has the highest value to the most stakeholders"*).

2.   Inform all stakeholders of the indicators, Evidence and targets for each Project, Result, Uses and Benefit and reconfirm with them why it is important to collect this information:

a.   It can be time-consuming, expensive and irritating to collect performance information, so people can be unenthusiastic about collecting it either if they are not going to use it themselves or if they are not convinced that someone else will use it

b.   For example, I know of a number of school teachers who have left the profession because the level of performance monitoring is so onerous and there is minimal Evidence that the information they collect and send to 'the powers that be' is ever used for any fruitful purpose.

c.   Stakeholders need to be motivated to collect measurement information because it is generally a tedious and unrewarding task. We have found that stakeholders are most motivated if they are collecting information on indicators that *they can use themselves* to improve their SubStrategies. They are motivated to a lesser extent by being compelled/paid to collect information for other stakeholders. We therefore recommend an initial focus on determining what indicators are most useful for the immediate performance management of SubStrategies and, where possible, use this same information for reporting to other stakeholders, rather than creating a parallel set of indicators and reports for other stakeholders.

3. Monitor the performance indicators and the cause-and-effect Evidence sufficiently often to underpin decision making to improve the performance of existing strategies in Stage 7 and to improve or create new strategies in Stage 9:

    a. Design the information collection, consolidation and reporting process so that the information is readily accessible for decision making.

    b. Always bear in mind *how* and *why* and *by whom* the information is going to be used, then collect and package it so as to increase its relevance and clarity for guiding ongoing decision making.

    c. The PRUB-Logic structure provides a rigorous framework for identifying exactly where to undertake monitoring:

        i.   Collect information on 'lead indicators' from Projects (progress information – efficiency) and Results (information on the consequences of Project processes – effectiveness).

        ii. Collect information on 'lag indicators' from Uses (progress information – efficiency) and Benefits (information on the consequences of Use processes – effectiveness).

        iii. Collect cause-and-effect information on the Links between: Projects and Results; Results and Uses; Uses and Benefits. As noted earlier, cause-and-effect Evidence requires 4 pieces of data:

            1. the initial state of the causative parameter;
            2. the final state of the causative parameter;

3.   the initial state of the parameter that is being caused to change;

4.   the final state of the parameter that is being caused to change.

iv.   Only robust cause-and-effect Evidence provides a basis for confident decision making as it makes clear what changes in the causative parameter are causing what changes in the parameter that is being caused to change. Performance management data on its own does not do this – it simply records that status of a parameter. This reinforces the need to collect genuine cause-and-effect *Evidence* about the existing SubStrategies, not just performance management *data*.

4.   Decision makers make wise, performance-enhancing decisions based on reliable performance monitoring information and on cause-and-effect Evidence:

a.   Reliable and robust information underpins robust decisions.

b.   In this respect, it can reasonably be argued that this fourth step of decision making should *guide* the selection of indicators and targets in order to enable good decision making.

c.   Crucially, decision makers need to carefully evaluate performance monitoring information to distinguish between the following:

i.   Data – mere numbers which do not indicate anything to guide decisions

ii.   Indicators – numbers which indicate 'something' which may influence decisions.

iii.   Correlations – changes that follow initial changes and which may or may not have been caused by the initial changes. These can guide decisions depending on the perceived strength of the correlation but should usually be followed up with more information to check if the correlation is merely a correlation or is Evidence of cause-and-effect.

      iv.   Cause-and-effect Evidence – information that confirms that some change *definitely* caused some other change and which is the most useful information for making decisions.

d.   It is essential to remember H. L. Menken's important observation that we quoted earlier: "for every problem there is a solution that is obvious, plausible and wrong". Performance monitoring frequently produces information that appears to point to 'obvious' solutions and 'obvious' process changes which actually made the process worse. So, making decisions based on performance monitoring information therefore requires considerable process control skills and experience to avoid the pitfall of 'obvious, plausible and wrong' decisions

e.   Therefore, to test if the decisions will lead to enhanced performance it is best to *Validate* them by updating the relevant PRUB-based SubStrategies with the newly decided actions and checking that they meet the three standards of strategy *Validation*:

      i.   they are logical (the PRUB-Logic-based SubStrategy makes sense);

      ii.   they will definitely work (there is compelling Evidence for the Links in the SubStrategy);

      iii.   they are Worth it (the SubStrategy has positive Global Worth and Motivational Worth).

5.   Project teams implement the new, performance-enhancing decisions:

a.   Once the decisions have been translated into *Validated* SubStrategies it will be clear to project managers what actions need to be taken. Additional resources may be required and these will need to have been considered in the decision-making process.

b.   It is essential to continue to monitor the parameters that led to the new decisions to check that the implementation of the decisions is in fact improving processes and producing more effective Results and Benefits and to make and implement further decisions if required.

Demonstration of Stage 8 actions

We will now apply these principles of PRUB-based performance management to the hypothetical Pingo River strategy as defined by the Aspirational Strategy in Figure 11.2.

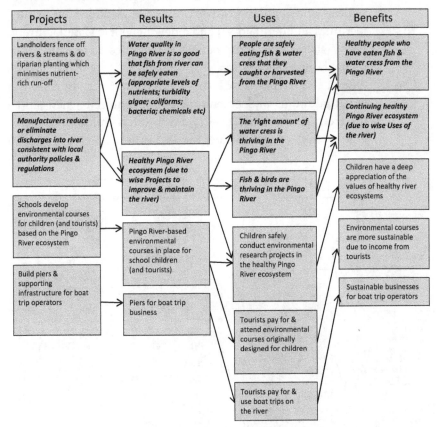

Figure 11.2   **Hypothetical Aspirational-level SubStrategy on environmentally sound Uses of the Pingo River showing (in *bold italics*) the Aspirational-level sub-SubStrategy relating *primarily* to the second Project: "Manufacturers reduce or eliminate discharges into river consistent with local authority policies and regulations".**

1.   For operational-level performance management we will now work with the hypothetical sub-SubStrategy relating to the 2nd high-level Project of: "Manufacturers reduce or eliminate

discharges into river consistent with local authority policies and regulations" as highlighted in Figure 11.2. At the operational level, this sub-SubStrategy would hypothetically be expanded into something like Figure 11.3.

2.   Figure 11.3 shows the original Project #2 expanded into 3 Operational-level Projects with one new Result ("Cost-effective policies and regulations in place and understood by manufacturers and regulators") and a new Benefit ("Manufacturers have a stronger legal right and 'social licence' to operate") but an unchanged set of Uses.

3.   One of the strengths of PRUB-Logic is that very often, only small additions and amendments are required when shifting from Aspirational-level down through Guidance-level to Operational-level SubStrategies.

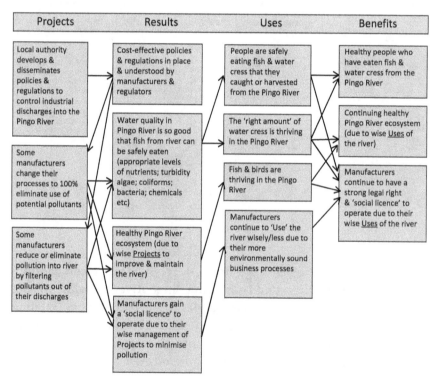

Figure 11.3   **Hypothetical Operational-level *sub*-SubStrategy on the second Project from the high-level Strategy: "Manufacturers reduce or eliminate discharges into river consistent with local authority policies and regulations".**

4.   PRUB-Logic provides a 'home' for performance monitoring information, i.e. within each Project, Result, Uses and Benefit. The *lead* indicators of progress in this example of the Pingo River relate to Projects and Results. Hypothetically, *some* of them could be as shown in Table 11.1. This list is illustrative, not exhaustive, and shows some possible *lead* indicators of *progress* for Projects and Results from the hypothetical Pingo River SubStrategy.

5.   Similarly, the *lag* indicators that measure *success* in this example of the Pingo River relate to Uses and Benefit. Hypothetically, some of them could be as shown in Table 11.2. This list is illustrative, not exhaustive, and shows some possible *lag* indicators for a Use and a Benefit from the hypothetical Pingo River SubStrategy.

6.   The above discussion and tables address the first task in Stage 8, ie. Determine if the *contractually specified indicators and targets are still relevant for monitoring and managing individual SubStrategies and for monitoring and managing the interactions between SubStrategies and agree on a final set of indicators and targets.*

7.   The second step of: *Inform all stakeholders of the indicators and targets for each Project, Result, Uses and Benefits* should be straightforward but will almost inevitably receive some push-back from manufacturers who believe that the policies and regulations are unrealistically stringent.

8.   Ultimately, decisions on the standards that must be achieved are likely to be political issues in which 'the powers that be' need to balance the desire for a healthy Pingo River with a parallel desire to permit manufacturers to continue to contribute to the economic well-being of the river catchment.

9.   The third step in Stage 8 of: *Monitor the indicators correctly and sufficiently frequently to underpin decision making to correct or improve performance* needs to determine how frequently and with what rigour to monitor the indicators in order to effectively enable the fourth step: *Decision makers make wise, performance-enhancing decisions based on reliable performance monitoring information.*

10.   In the Pingo River example, measurements of the indicators for the second Project and second Result are likely to be particularly valuable to key decision makers because they provide

Table 11.1   Some possible *lead* indicators of *progress* for a Project and Result from the hypothetical Pingo River SubStrategy

Project or Result	Possible Indicators (I) and Targets (T) for Performance Management	Comments
Project: local authority develops and disseminates policies and regulations to control industrial discharges into the Pingo River	1. I = % completion of policies and regulations; T = 100% within 3 months 2. I = % of policy budget spent to date; T = 70% at 6 months and 100% at 12 months	The performance monitoring indicators for this Project relate to monitoring *progress* in a *process* so they monitor *actions*
Result: cost-effective policies and regulations in place and understood by manufacturers and regulators	1. I = the likely cost-effectiveness of the policies and regulations; T = at least 95% likely to be accepted and complied with by manufacturers because they are cost-effective 2. I = % of manufacturers who have received the new policies/regulations; T = 100% within 7 months 3. I = % of manufacturers who demonstrably understand the policies/regulations; T = 90% within 12 months	Regulations must not only be created but they must be demonstrably cost-effective and disseminated and the stakeholders who are affected must understand them and be prepared to comply with them. Performance monitoring indicators for this Result relate to monitoring a *consequence* of a process so they monitor *things*
Project: some manufacturers change their processes to 100% eliminate use of potential pollutants	1. I = % of previously polluting manufacturers who are changing their processes to eliminate polluting discharges; T = 50% within 24 months and 80% within 5 years	This lead indicator indicates whether or not currently polluting manufacturers are responding to the new regulations. It indicates where manufacturers are heading but it doesn't yet indicate whether or not polluting discharges will actually be eliminated
Result: water quality in Pingo River is so good that fish from the river can be safely eaten (appropriate levels of nutrients; turbidity algae; coliforms; bacteria; chemicals etc)	1. I = % of manufacturers no longer discharging any pollutants; T = 80% within 5 years 2. I = levels of the key water quality indicators (nutrients; turbidity; coliforms; chemicals etc): T = the levels that have been set in the policies and regulations	The first lead indicator is a crucial one because it directly monitors the consequences of manufacturers' process-improvement actions on the quality of discharges. The subsequent indicators should confirm the effectiveness of the eliminated polluting discharges

Table 11.2   Some possible *lag* indicators of *success* for a Use and a Benefit from the hypothetical Pingo River SubStrategy

Use or Benefit	Possible Indicators (I) and Targets (T) for Performance Management	Comments
Use: people are safely eating fish and watercress that they caught or harvested from the Pingo River	I. I = the number of people catching fish, harvesting watercress and eating them; T = 100/week (fishing) and 30/week (harvesting) between September and May	While the Use referred to people *safely* eating the fish and cress, safety and its consequence of good health are actually Benefits – the Use is simply the 'neutral' actions of catching/harvesting/eating
Benefit: healthy people who have eaten fish and watercress from the Pingo River	I. I = the % of people who have eaten fish/cress from the Pingo River who have become ill as a consequence; T = 0.1% within 2 years and 0.01% within 5 years	It may take some time for the Pingo River's health to be good enough for fish/cress to be safely eaten so 100% safety/health cannot be immediately achieved. Even in the long term, accidental discharges may occur plus more birds may move into the healthier river and increase faecal coliform levels to the extent that the fish and cress (sometimes) become unsafe to eat. So, targets need to be realistic *and* be flexible in order to accommodate future changes in the river

early indications, and predictors of, overall success with the subset of the strategy dealing with eliminating polluting discharges from a substantial percentage of manufacturers.

11.   In contrast, measurements of indicators for the first Project and first Result are likely to be of interest to just the project manager and project sponsor because all the other stakeholders will reasonably assume that these people have the regulation-developing Project 'under control'.

12.   The second Result is an Orphan Result – it will not be used by end-users and it does not actually do anything to improve water quality. It is an essential Result but it will not be seen by most stakeholders as worth their while to monitor it.

13.   In contrast, many more stakeholders will be interested in the performance of the second Result relating to the cleanliness of discharges and the health of the river.

14.   The final step in Stage 8 of the Pingo River example: *Project teams implement the new, performance-enhancing decisions* relies on actions that in general are 'upstream' of where the

monitoring information was collected. So, for the second Result, if the target of *80% of previously polluting manufacturers are changing their processes to eliminate polluting discharges within 5 years* is not being achieved then this cannot be fixed by changing the Result. It can only be fixed by going 'upstream' to the Project of: *some manufacturers change their processes to 100% eliminate use of potential pollutants* and encouraging more manufacturers to move faster on their pollution-elimination projects. This may require additional Projects and Results to motivate this to happen.

15. Similarly, for the first Use of: *People are safely eating fish and watercress that they caught or harvested from the Pingo River*, if the targets are not being met it may mean 1, 2 or more things need to happen 'upstream', e.g.:

   a. the river is not clean enough for people to want to catch fish and harvest watercress (in which case the clean-up needs to be accelerated by speeding up the Projects to reduce pollution); and/or

   b. the river may be clean enough but people do not know that so they do not go to the river to catch fish and harvest cress (in which case a *new* Project may be required to tell people about the newly healthy river);

   c. the river may be clean enough but people are not actually using it because they just want the *option* of using it or they believe that clean rivers are inherently 'a good thing' (in which case no action is required).

16. This is where Evidence of cause-and-effect needs to be considered. In this example: was the lack of Use caused by an ongoing unhealthy river ecosystem or was it caused by people not knowing that the river was now cleaner or was it caused by people not being interested in actually fishing and harvesting cress?

17. The performance monitoring of the indicators of water quality would show whether or not the river was or was not healthy. To determine if people know about that and if they wanted to catch fish or harvest cress it would be necessary to add a new Project along the lines of: "survey potential river users to determine their understanding of the river water quality and their desires to catch fish or harvest cress". If the survey

identified a lack of knowledge of the river and its potential Uses, then a new Project could be added to help inform users.

Accountabilities in Stage 8

1.   Suppliers are primarily responsible for the monitoring and acting on the efficiency with which their Projects produce Results.
2.   Purchasers are primarily responsible for monitoring and responding to the efficiency with which Uses use Results.
3.   Purchasers are also primarily responsible for monitoring and responding to the effectiveness of the Benefits.

Comments

1.   PRUB-Logic shows exactly where performance monitoring should be undertaken (within Projects, Results, Uses and Benefits).
2.   PRUB-Logic guides performance management by showing where changes need to be made if performance targets are not being achieved i.e. one step upstream: if Benefits are not being achieved, then fix the Uses; if Uses are not being achieved, then fix the Results; if the Results are not being achieved, then fix the Projects.
3.   PRUB-Logic also defines exactly where to ask questions about cause-and-effect Evidence, i.e. on the Links between Projects and Results, between Results and Uses, and between Uses and Benefits.
4.   As a consequence, performance monitoring and management using PRUB defines the smallest number of measurements that are necessary to enable effective performance management decision making.

The information on performance generated in Stage 8 underpins the overall review and updating of the strategy in Stage 9 (Chapter 12).

Chapter 12

Stage 9 – Review and update strategies

Reminder: Our purpose is to *enable and motivate Uses to create Benefits*

PRUB Mantra #1: *Only Uses create Benefits*

PRUB Mantra #2: Uses need the *right* Results or they won't happen

PRUB Mantra #3: Projects, Results, Uses and Benefits must be Linked with compelling Evidence

PRUB Mantra #4: SubStrategies must be Globally and Motivationally Worth it

PRUB Mantra #5: Invest in the 'best' SubStrategies

PRUB Mantra #6: Contracts define who does what for what rewards and Benefits

PRUB Mantra #7: Implement with confidence

PRUB Mantra #8: You do not fatten the pig by measuring it. You must take action on performance measurements

PRUB Mantra #9: The world is complex. Things change. Update your SubStrategies accordingly.

What is Stage 9?

Stage 9 consists of regularly reviewing the SubStrategies (Stage 3) and their implementation and performance management (Stages 7 and 8) to check that they are effective and if necessary updating them. If done rapidly and repeatedly, this iterative process can in many circumstances correlate with 'Agile' development.

Although Stage 9 could reasonably be perceived as the final stage in a 9-stage process, the 9 stages are better thought of as a set of significant actions that constantly inform each other on a continuous cycle.

In contrast to Stage 8 which regularly monitored and managed the *efficiency* of implementation of *current* SubStrategies, Stage 9 reviews the overall strategy itself to check if it is still the most *effective strategy* and updates it to make it more appropriate and effective, or even replaces it with a better strategy. Stages 8 and 9 invariably overlap but for clarity they are discussed separately here.

So, Stage 8 focuses on *efficiency of implementation of current strategies* and Stage 9 focuses on whether or not the *current SubStrategies are effective and if they should be updated or replaced with new ones*.

By retaining copies of each stage of evolution of the SubStrategies, Stage 9 also provides an audit trail of evolving SubStrategies which highlight what worked and what did not work so that lessons that have been learned are not lost.

What Stage 9 will achieve in order to support the other eight stages

1. Stage 9 will produce a thorough summary of exactly where the current SubStrategies worked well or worked badly so as to guide the development of better SubStrategies.
2. Success/failure will be evident if actual Results, Uses and Benefits are the same as/differ from those predicted by the current SubStrategies.
3. Such successes/failures will have been caused or at least influenced by the 'upstream' factors in the PRUB-sequence.
4. For example:
    a. If the current Projects and Results have been correctly implemented and the anticipated Uses have happened but there is nevertheless still a failure of a Benefit being achieved then this will be because the Uses were not the right ones to create that Benefit. Therefore, a different Use needs to be designed into a revised strategy.
    b. Similarly, if a Result has not been Used as planned, this will have been caused by the wrong or insufficient Result – so different or additional Results needs to be created via revised Projects within a revised SubStrategy (see Figure 12.1).

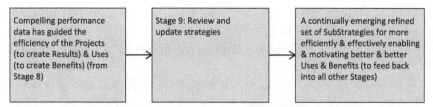

| Compelling performance data has guided the efficiency of the Projects (to create Results) & Uses (to create Benefits) (from Stage 8) | → | Stage 9: Review and update strategies | → | A continually emerging refined set of SubStrategies for more efficiently & effectively enabling & motivating better & better Uses & Benefits (to feed back into all other Stages) |

Figure 12.1   The precursor to Stage 9, Stage 9 itself and what Stage 9 must feed back into all other stages.

WHY IS STAGE 9 IMPORTANT?

1. Because the world is complex and constantly changing, few strategies achieve 100% of what they set out to achieve. Strategies need to evolve to match the changing circumstances, whether they be changes in end-user requirements, changes in the regulatory environment, changes in resource availability or any other changes.

2. Although occasionally it will be appropriate to throw out an old strategy and replace it with something completely different (an expensive option), more often it is appropriate to tweak existing strategies to better align them with the changing world.

3. The performance monitoring information from Stage 8 will have generated information which shows exactly where existing SubStrategies are failing (or succeeding) and hence where it is necessary to tweak or upgrade the overall strategy.

4. While Stage 8 focused on implementing the current SubStrategies as efficiently as possible, it may not have picked up on the fact that the *wrong* SubStrategies were being implemented. So, no matter how well and efficiently the current SubStrategies were project-managed, they still would not generate the desired Benefits.

Summary of the start-to-finish action sequence for Stage 9

Ideally, this review process will start by reviewing whether or not the desired Benefits were or are being achieved. The key questions that need to be asked are:

1.   If the SubStrategies created the desired Benefits, would refined SubStrategies enable more/better Benefits for lower cost?

2.   If the SubStrategies did not enable and motivate Uses to create the desired Benefits then:

   a.   Did the Uses happen as expected but the Benefits did not arise?

   b.   Did the Uses not happen as expected so the Benefits did not arise?

3.   If the SubStrategies did not enable and motivate the desired Uses then:

   a.   Were the desired Results available but did not get used?

   b.   Did the intended Results not get created?

   c.   Were other factors, including negative factors, at play that reduced the viability and the Global and Motivational Worths of the SubStrategies?

Explanation of the start-to-finish action sequence for Stage 9

SubStrategies based on PRUB-Logic provide an ideal basis for strategy review by offering a structured sequence of steps from Projects through Results, Uses and Benefits which can be analysed individually and collectively. They also provide a succinct and precise framework for identifying and quantifying performance management indicators and targets and knowing exactly where they fit in the process from Projects through Results and Uses to Benefits.

Ideally, the strategy review process will start by reviewing whether or not the desired Benefits were or are being achieved. The key questions that need to be asked are:

1.   If the SubStrategies created the desired Benefits, would refined SubStrategies enable more/better Benefits for lower cost?

   a.   It would be common for strategies to evolve as they are implemented and as more information is collected. For example, predicting the *actual Uses and level of Uses* is always challenging so the reality is likely to diverge from the predictions. This will frequently require a refining of the Results so that they better motivate and enable the Uses to create the Benefits.

2.   If the SubStrategies did not create the desired Benefits then:

    a.   Did the Uses happen as expected but the Benefits did not arise? If so, then *the wrong set of Uses was chosen in the SubStrategies*, so you need to enable better/different Uses:

        i.   Just as it is challenging to predict *actual* Uses and *actual* levels of Uses, it is challenging to predict *actual* Benefits that *will* emerge from the Uses. If the forecast, desired Benefits are not emerging from the Uses, then either the Results need to be changed to enable and motivate different Uses that will in fact lead to the Benefits or it may be that the stakeholders accept that there are still Worthwhile, but different, Benefits emerging and that that is OK.

    b.   Did the Uses not happen as expected so the Benefits did not arise? If so then *the wrong or insufficient Results were created that did not enable/motivate the Uses*, so you need to create better/different Results:

        i.   As with 1a above, it is challenging to accurately predict Uses and Benefits. If Uses are not happening, then it is not possible to fix the Uses. It is necessary to fix the Results so that the improved/ new Results *do* enable and motivate the Uses to create the desired (and/or new) Benefits.

3.   If the SubStrategies did not enable the desired Uses then:

    a.   Were the desired Results available but did not get used? If so, then *the wrong/insufficient Results were chosen in the SubStrategies*, so you need to create better/different/more Results – by creating better/different/more Projects. If the right physical Results were not Used, then it may be that they were *insufficient*, e.g. the right physical Results might have been available but maybe no-one knew about them (so a marketing Project-Result needs to be added) or maybe they were not accessible (so maybe new transport/parking options need to be added) or maybe they were not genuinely desired by the users (even if the users originally said they would use the Results).

b.   Did the intended Results not get created? If so, then *the wrong Projects were run*, so you need to run better/different Projects to produce the intended Results.

c.   Were other factors, including negative factors, at play that reduced the viability and Global and Motivational Worth of the SubStrategies?

Demonstration of Stage 9 actions

Let us review the hypothetical operational-level Pingo River sub-Sub-Strategy as shown in Figure 12.2.

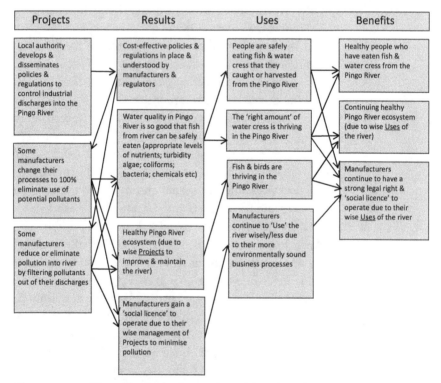

Figure 12.2   Hypothetical Operational-level sub-SubStrategy which expanded on the high-level Project: "Manufacturers reduce or eliminate discharges into river consistent with local authority policies and regulations" from the high-level Pingo River strategy.

1.   Let us consider some hypothetical examples of how this sub-SubStrategy might fail:

    a.   People may have become ill from eating fish or water-cress in the river. Why? Maybe the first two Uses did happen as anticipated but maybe the third Use: "Fish and birds are thriving in the Pingo River" causes high level of faecal coliforms from birds and this is what led to the people becoming ill. So, no matter what the manufacturers did to minimise pollution, the fish and watercress would still not be safe to eat. In this case, and depending on many other factors, maybe a new Project such as a cull of birds would be required. This happens from time to time in New Zealand in catchments which become overrun with Canadian geese. In other rivers, people like the birds so much that they tolerate the resultant 'natural' pollution and choose not to harvest food from the river.

    b.   Similarly, people may be become ill due to the removal of pollution from manufacturers being insufficient to clean up the river. For example, run-off from roads (oils; dog droppings) and from residential and rural properties (fertilisers; household chemicals) may be major contributors to ecosystem ill-health. To fix this in order to achieve the desired Uses and Benefits it would be necessary to add new Projects to better manage such run-offs.

    c.   Benefit #3 may not have been achieved: ("Manufacturers have a stronger legal right and 'social licence' to operate") because no-one knew that manufacturers had substantially improved their operations. This would logically lead to the creation of a new Project along the lines of: "Raise public awareness of manufacturers' good stewardship of Pingo River water".

2.   In all 3 examples, PRUB-Logic-based SubStrategies provide a robust thinking structure for identifying successes (Benefits being achieved) and failures (Benefits not being achieved) and then systematically working upstream through the Uses, Results and Projects in the SubStrategy to identify weaknesses or where additions may be needed.

3.   It is then straightforward to update and re-Validate PRUB-Logic-based SubStrategies by editing/adding Projects, Results and Uses Benefits so that they have the potential to actually achieve the desired initial (and/or new) Benefits.

4.   This does not mean that the updated SubStrategies will automatically be implemented because there may be insufficient resources to do so. However, the new SubStrategies will provide a basis for developing robust business cases for securing the necessary resources to implement the updated strategies to ultimately achieve the desired Benefits.

Accountabilities in Stage 9

Purchasers are primarily accountable for funding effective and efficient strategies so Stage 9 is *primarily* the responsibility of purchasers. Certainly, purchasers are likely to involve all stakeholders in any refinement of the overall strategy but purchasers are responsible for making this happen (see Chapter 3).

Comments

1.   PRUB-based SubStrategies provide a clear and succinct information framework for diagnosing the success or failure of strategies and for identifying exactly what modified/new Projects, Results and Uses are required to generate the initially desired and/or new Benefits.

2.   They also provide a succinct and precise framework for identifying and quantifying performance management indicators and targets and knowing exactly where they fit in the process sequence from Projects through Results and Uses to Benefits.

3.   As noted earlier and worth repeating here, it is crucial that the *development/refinement* of a strategy should not be confused with *decisions on whether or not to implement* a strategy. A Validated strategy or set of SubStrategies defines what *can* genuinely happen and what *will* be Worth doing but decisions on whether or not to allocate resources to such strategies are *outside the strategy*. This is important because if resource

limitations are introduced too soon into a strategy develop-
ment/review process they can seriously limit thinking.

4.   By designing a strategy without too may initial resource
      constraints it is possible to define clearly what needs doing
      and then *other stakeholders* can step in and offer to help. In the
      case of the wilding pines referred to earlier, members of rec-
      reational groups offered to cut down the wilding pines dur-
      ing annual trips into the high country. The Department of
      Conservation was able to provide tools; local authorities pro-
      vided buses to take the volunteers into the high country; and
      local farmers provided free barbeques at the end of the day.
      So, the (unexpected) resources to implement this SubStrategy
      emerged *after* it was clear what needed doing (the SubStrategy
      itself).

5.   So, it is essential to create and review strategies without
      assuming limited resources because once strategies and
      their Benefits to multiple stakeholders are clear, unexpected
      resources can often turn up to enable the strategies to be
      implemented.

Chapter 13 now summarises PRUB-Logic and PRUB-Accountability
and then provides checklists for each of the 9 stages as handy guides for
practitioners.

Chapter 13
Summary

This chapter summarises PRUB-Logic and PRUB-Accountabilities and then provides practitioners with handy, checklists of each stage in the OpenStrategies system.

What is the challenge that PRUB addresses?

Through conversations with several thousand people in the public, private and voluntary sectors we have deduced that less than 20% (and probably less than 10%) of strategies come even close to achieving their intended impact.

Why is this?

We have concluded that:

- The real world is complex (full of unknown-unknowns as defined by Snowden and Boone – *A Leader's Framework for Decision Making* by David J. Snowden and Mary E. Boone, Harvard Business Review R0711C) and full of uncertainties.
- However, strategies and actions must necessarily be simple (known-knowns), i.e. you have to know what Projects you are going to do even if you are not 100% sure what the Results of your actions will be, if/how they will be used and if/how they will create Benefits.
- It can be challenging to translate between the complexity of the real world and the simplicity necessary for effective actions.
- Complexity includes multiple stakeholders; multiple agendas; multiple and diverse end-users, suppliers, purchasers and strategic ideas; the need for many different people to

simultaneously understand and implement different levels of strategies.

- Strategies and business systems must work with the fact that humans have cognitive limits:
  - Miller's law states that humans can hold just 7 +/– 2 ideas in their heads at any one time.
  - Through our observations of thousands of stakeholders engaged with many strategies, we have deduced that humans can cope with just 15+/–5 concepts in diagrammatic form (Driver's law: we welcome feedback on this deduction).
- So, strategies need to be 'chunked' into bite-sized units of 15+/–5 concepts.
- Stakeholders often have minimal 'strategy' knowledge, so they need an ultra-simple strategy language which produces:
  - *the smallest amount of strategy information that has the highest value to the most stakeholders.*
- The world keeps changing so most strategies need to be constantly updated. So any strategy system must be flexible enough to be quickly reviewed and updated and for all stakeholders to know about the updates.
- There is therefore a need for a start-to-finish system which simultaneously addresses *all* the above challenges.
- This requires a common strategy language that everyone understands and which works in every one of the 9 stages described in this book.
- There are important distinctions between:
  - identifying an issue;
  - quantifying an issue;
  - contractually specifying what will be done about an issue;
  - actually doing what is required including measuring and monitoring an issue.
- Someone needs to be accountable for all these aspects of strategy development and implementation and that accountability needs to be clear and closely linked to the strategies themselves.
- Strategies need to be 'Worth it' if they are to be implemented. They need to be:

- Globally Worth it: the value of all the Benefits must be greater than all the Project costs plus all the Use costs that will be incurred to enable the Benefits;
- Motivationally Worth it: each stakeholder who needs to contribute to the strategy needs to gain enough Worth to be motivated to make that contribution.
- So, in complex multi-stakeholder environments, the challenge is to have a system which:
  - simultaneously addresses *all* the above issues;
  - identifies the *smallest amount of strategic information that has the highest value to the most stakeholders*;
  - captures this information in a form that can be easily and continually:
    - disseminated to all stakeholders.
    - understood by all stakeholders.
    - directly implemented by all stakeholders.

This book defines such a system (the OpenStrategies system based on PRUB-Logic) and demonstrates how it enables and seamlessly interlinks each of the 9 stages from the generation of initial ideas through to strategy development, implementation, review and updating. The 9 stages are:

1. Stage 1: Understand Uses and Benefits
2. Stage 2: Understand Projects and Results
3. Stage 3: Develop Evidence-based strategies
4. Stage 4: Validate SubStrategies by determining their Worth
5. Stage 5: Make investment decisions
6. Stage 6: Create performance-based contracts
7. Stage 7: Implement strategies
8. Stage 8: Performance-manage strategies
9. Stage 9: Review and update strategies

Different stakeholders will be involved in each of the 9 stages and so they need to produce information in each stage that suits the audience in the subsequent stage. Therefore, each stage needs to be understandable by the stakeholders in the previous stage, in the stage itself and in the subsequent stage.

This in turn means that stakeholders involved in any or all 9 of the above stages must *all speak the same strategy language* so they can most effectively communicate and interlink their respective activities.

Ideally, this means that *the same or similar PRUB-Logic information will ideally be used and reused for 9 separate but seamlessly interlinked purposes* so there is no need to learn a new set of jargon for each stage.

This is exactly what the OpenStrategies system, based on PRUB-Logic, does.

The main features of PRUB-Logic

PRUB-Logic exactly represents reality. PRUB-Logic precisely represents the real-world sequence common to all initiatives:

> *Create assets (outputs) that enable and motivate Uses to create Benefits (outcomes)* i.e., *Run **P**rojects to create **R**esults that enable and motivate **U**ses to create **B**enefits*

The Results must be both necessary and sufficient to enable and motivate Uses to create Benefits.

PRUB-Logic represents:

> *The smallest amount of strategic information that has the highest value for the most stakeholders*

PRUB-Logic is easy to understand by almost all stakeholders because it is clear and succinct and aligns with humans' cognitive limits, especially our experience that humans can effectively comprehend just 15+/–5 concepts when presented in diagrammatic format.

PRUB-Logic-based strategies can easily be 'chunked' into several levels of 'SubStrategies' (e.g., 'Aspirational-level'; 'Guidance-level'; and 'Operational-level').

Strategies based on PRUB-Logic guide the development of strategies (follow the 'BURP' sequence, often starting strategic thinking by defining the Uses) and are simultaneously directly implementable (follow the PRUB sequence).

PRUB-Logic confirms that there are no shortcuts from inputs (Projects) to outcomes (Benefits). To be successful, implementation of a strategy/contract *must* follow the sequence: *"Projects create Results that enable and motivate Uses to create Benefits"*.

Crucially, *only Uses create Benefits*. Projects *never* create Benefits/outcomes.

Suppliers can only *influence*, not *ensure* Uses and Benefits.

Similarly, project managers cannot 'realise Benefits' – only Uses create Benefits. Certainly, project managers can lead Projects which create effective, necessary and sufficient Results which will enable and motivate end-users to implement Uses and in so doing to create Benefits. So, project managers can 'control Projects and Results' but can only 'influence Uses and Benefits'.

Figure 13.1 summarises the actions (Projects and Uses) and their consequences (Results and Benefits) associated with each of these 9 stages.

PRUB-Logic precisely locates performance management information (within each Project, Result, Use and Benefit) and cause-and-effect Evidence (on the Links between the Projects, Results, Uses and Benefits). PRUB-Logic also identifies that:

- Measures of Projects and Uses are measures of *Efficiency*.
- Measures of Results and Benefits are measures of *Effectiveness*.
- Measures of Projects and Results are measures of lead indicators and they give an indication of *progress*.
- Measures of Uses and Benefits are measures of lag indicators and they give an indication of *success*.

PRUB-Logic enables the succinct chunking of strategic information:

1. As individual SubStrategies of 15+/–5 concepts (Projects; Results; Uses; Benefits).
2. As hierarchies of SubStrategies (layers of sub-SubStrategies with ideally no more than 15+/–5 sub-SubStrategies in each layer).
3. Information further 'chunked' so it is relevant to each of the 9 stages.

So not only can stakeholders associated with each of the 9 stages communicate with stakeholders associated with the stages that are immediately before or after their own stage, they can also communicate with stakeholders who are leading any and all of the 9 stages. This is essential because each and every stage is dependent on all the other stages in an ongoing cycle of idea generation, strategy *Validation*, implementation, review and updating.

The world is complex (unknown-unknowns) but actions must necessarily be simple (known-knowns).

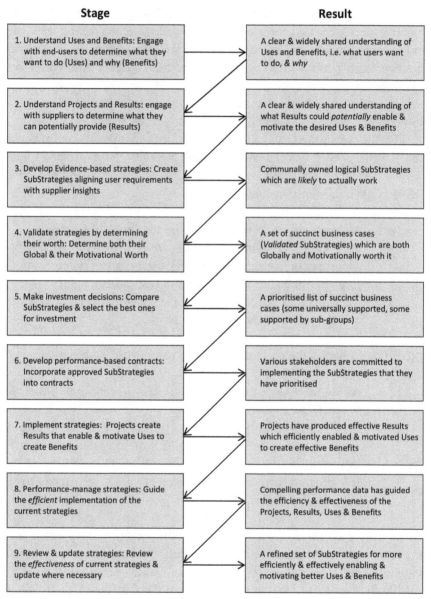

Figure 13.1   The actions (Projects and Uses) and their consequences (Results and Benefits) associated with each of the 9 stages in the OpenStrategies system.

PRUB-Logic represents the 'known-knowns' (simple actions) while acknowledging that the Results, Uses and Benefits derived from implementing SubStrategies may turn out to be different from expectations due to the ever-changing complexity of the real world. But this does not change the fact that each and every action must necessarily *always* be 'simple' as defined by PRUB-Logic-based SubStrategies.

Although PRUB-Logic was developed for large, complex, multi-stakeholder environments it is equally applicable to small strategic initiatives by single people.

Accountability

The term 'accountability' is commonly used in two ways:

1.   'Accountable for' – i.e., being accountable for achieving what you said you were going to achieve.
2.   'Accountable to' – i.e., reporting to someone about whether you did or did not achieve anything.

Being 'accountable for' is overwhelmingly more important than being 'accountable to'. This is so important that in our world of PRUB-Logic we do not allow the concept of 'accountable to' and instead replace it with 'reporting to'.

'Being Accountable for achieving what you promised':

1.   This is, in our view, the only meaningful form of accountability.
2.   It focuses:
     a.   First, on what has been achieved; and
     b.   Second, on who was supposed to achieve it.
3.   It therefore describes concrete facts about whether or not what stakeholders want achieved has actually been achieved and this is the overall purpose of strategies, i.e., to *achieve* things, especially to *enable and motivate Uses to create Benefits*.
4.   If relevant stakeholders have achieved what they set out to achieve, then they have been accountable, whether or not they

report on it – so 'being accountable to' someone is somewhat irrelevant.

5. If relevant stakeholders have *not* achieved what they set out to achieve then this nonachievement is what will matter to most stakeholders. Certainly, most stakeholders will want someone 'held to account' but the key issue will be that the desired achievements weren't achieved – so again, 'being accountable to' someone is less important to most stakeholders than 'being accountable for' achievements.

'Being accountable to ...'

1. Frequently, it is too easy to claim that you have 'been accountable' because you have 'been accountable *to*' someone by sending them a report or having a meeting with whoever you were 'accountable to', even if you have not achieved what you promised to achieve. *This is not 'being accountable', it is merely 'reporting'* and has minimal value relative to the desired achievements.

2. Because 'being accountable to' is seldom well defined and seldom leads to any significant action for failure to 'be accountable for' it is too often pointless. This frequently results in people who do not achieve what they promised to achieve receiving merely a slap on the wrist with a wet bus ticket, while all those stakeholders who were supposed to gain benefits from what was supposed to be achieved getting nothing.

3. Also, 'being accountable to' focuses on the person being reported to and less on what is being reported on and whether or not it demonstrates 'accountability for achievements'.

4. 'Accountable to' is therefore frequently an all-too-easy way out for people to claim they have been 'accountable' even when they have not achieved what they said they would, so in practice 'being accountable to' is frequently completely ineffective.

So, in the world of OpenStrategies we do not allow the concept of 'accountable to'. We use 'accountable for' and 'reporting to'. We believe this is profoundly important.

PRUB-Accountability

There are 4 types of accountabilities, each with 4 stages, giving a 16-box matrix:

The 4 types of accountability are:

1. Project Efficiency.
2. Result Effectiveness.
3. Use Efficiency.
4. Benefit Effectiveness.

The 4 stages of accountability are:

1. Identify and define what *could* be measured and managed.
2. Select what *must* be measured and managed.
3. Contractually specify what *must* be measured and managed.
4. Actually measure and manage these factors.

The *default* responsibility for the various types of accountability and stages of accountability are as shown in Table 13.1.

Table 13.1 Default accountabilities in the PRUB-Accountability matrix

Accountabilities for Effectiveness and Efficiency (E&E)	Project Efficiency (running Projects 'right')	Result Effectiveness (the right Result)	Use Efficiency (Uses happening 'right')	Benefit Effectiveness (the right Benefits)
Identify and Link desired E&E	Purchaser	Purchaser	Purchaser	Purchaser
Value and Prioritise desired E&E	Purchaser	Purchaser	Purchaser	Purchaser
Specify desired E&E	Supplier + purchaser	Supplier + purchaser	Purchaser	Purchaser
Implement, Performance-Manage and Confirm actual E&E	Supplier	Supplier	Purchaser	Purchaser

Project Efficiency and Result Effectiveness can be *managed*.

Use Efficiency and Benefit Effectiveness can only be *influenced*.

This influence is optimised by creating the right set of necessary and sufficient Results to *enable and motivate Uses to create Benefits*. So, Benefits effectiveness is 100% dependent on Results effectiveness (*Only* if the *right* Results are made available will the Benefits arise from the Uses).

Effectiveness-Accountability is primarily (but not solely) the responsibility of purchasers.

Project Efficiency-Accountability is primarily (but not solely) the responsibility of suppliers.

Figure 13.2 shows the steps that need to be taken (linearly and iteratively) to obtain and manage accountabilities throughout the 9 stages from an initial identification of end-users' needs through to defining, implementing and performance-managing solutions.

Toolkit summaries of each of the 9 stages

Reminder: Our purpose is *to enable and motivate Uses to create Benefits*.

PRUB Mantra #1: *Only Uses create Benefits*

PRUB Mantra #2: Uses need the *right* Results or they won't happen

PRUB Mantra #3: Projects, Results, Uses and Benefits must be Linked with compelling Evidence

PRUB Mantra #4: SubStrategies must be Globally and Motivationally Worth it

PRUB Mantra #5: Invest in the 'best' SubStrategies

PRUB Mantra #6: Contracts define who does what for what rewards and Benefits

PRUB Mantra #7: Implement with confidence

PRUB Mantra #8: You do not fatten the pig by measuring it. You must take action on performance measurements

PRUB Mantra #9: The world is complex. Things change. Update your SubStrategies accordingly

All 9 stages, starting with end-user engagement and ending with strategy review and updating, can be effectively defined and interlinked using *and reusing* the same PRUB-Logic-based SubStrategies, irrespective of the complexity of a situation.

In the following pages the 9 stages are summarised as ready-reference checklists for practitioners.

Stage	Accountabilities for this Stage
1. Understand Uses and Benefits: Determine what users want to do (Uses) and why (Benefits)	Identify Benefit-Effectiveness (P) &Use-Efficiency (P)
2. Understand Projects & Results: Determine what suppliers can create (Results)	Identify Result-Effectiveness (P) & Project-Efficiency (P)
3. Develop Evidence-based Strategies: Links Projects & Results to Uses & Benefits	Convincingly Link Result-Effectiveness to Use-Efficiency & Benefit-Effectiveness (P)
4. Validate strategies by determining their Global & Motivational Worths	Quantify value/significance of Project-Efficiency (P); Result-Effectiveness (P); Use-Efficiency (P); Benefit-Effectiveness (P)
5. Make investment decisions: Compare SubStrategies & select the best ones	Prioritise Project-Efficiency (P); Result-Effectiveness (P); Use-Efficiency (P); Benefits-Effectiveness (P)
6. Create performance-based contracts: Create contracts based on SubStrategies	Specify/negotiate Project-Efficiency (P/S); Result-Effectiveness (P/S); Use-Efficiency (P); Benefit-Effectiveness (P)
7. Implement strategies: Projects create Results & enable Uses to create Benefits	Efficiently run Projects (S) to produce Effective Results (S) which will be Efficiently Used (P) to create Effective Benefits (P)
8. Manage performance: Manage Projects → Results: *Influence* Uses → Benefits	*Monitor* & *Manage* Project-Efficiency & Result-Effectiveness (S): Monitor & *Influence* Use-Efficiency & Benefit-Effectiveness (P)
9. Review & update strategies: Improve Projects to create better Results, Uses & Benefits	Update Projects(S) to produce more Effectives Results (P), more Efficient Uses (P) & more Effective Benefits (P)

Figure 13.2 *Default* effectiveness and efficiency accountabilities as they relate to developing and implementing strategies and contracts. These accountabilities may be subcontracted to other parties. (P = Purchaser; S = Supplier).

Stage 1: Understand Uses and Benefits

WHAT IS STAGE 1?

Stage 1 consists of engaging with end-users in various ways in order to accurately understand what they want to *do* (Uses) and *why* they want to do them (Benefits/Motivations). The purpose in all cases must be to understand what users want to *do* and *why*.

WHAT STAGE 1 WILL ACHIEVE IN ORDER TO SUPPORT THE OTHER EIGHT STAGES

1. Essential: Stage 1 *must* generate a thorough (objective; quantified; verified) and documented understanding of what end-users will *actually do* (Uses) and *why* (Benefits). These Uses and Benefits could be proposed or they could be new Uses and Benefits to create a new strategy or existing Uses and Benefits which are being audited to improve an existing strategy.
2. Optional: Stage 1 may also document what end-users believe they need (a *necessary and sufficient set* of Results) in order to enable and motivate their Uses.

Stage 1 is therefore essential for focusing all stakeholders' minds on determining the actual requirements of end-users and not their assumed requirements.

THE START-TO-FINISH ACTION SEQUENCE FOR STAGE 1

Stage 1 requires the following actions:

1. Determine and agree on 'the problem/opportunity'.
2. Determine and agree on Values.
3. Determine and agree on Fundamental Principles which correlate with those Values.
4. Determine what users want to *do* (= Uses) and *why* (=Benefits/ motivations) and collate their answers as a set of *potential* Uses and Benefits.
5. Optionally: determine what products/services/infrastructure (i.e., Results) users think they need to enable and motivate

them to do the Uses to obtain the Benefits. We make this stage optional because once Uses and Benefits have been accurately identified, many of the necessary Results are obvious, albeit needing to be *Validated*.

6. Where possible, start collecting cause-and-effect Evidence that Results *will* be Used and that these Uses *will* generate the Benefits.

7. Add performance indicators as narratives associated with each box of information i.e. what will success look like for each Benefit, Use, Result and Project?

8. Cross-check that the desired Uses and Benefits align with the agreed Values and Fundamental Principles.

9. Ask other stakeholders how the potential Results and Uses will affect them and where appropriate add these effects into the emerging SubStrategy.

Stage 2: Understand projects and results

WHAT IS STAGE 2?

Stage 2 consists of engaging with suppliers and purchasers to learn how they believe they can create Results that will *enable and motivate Uses to create Benefits*.

WHAT STAGE 2 WILL ACHIEVE IN ORDER TO SUPPORT THE OTHER 8 STAGES

1. Stage 2 will produce a list of Projects which suppliers and other stakeholders *could* potentially undertake, which *will* produce Results which are necessary, sufficient and sufficiently attractive to end-users that they *will* be motivated to Use them to create Benefits. The Results could be products, services or infrastructure.
2. In Stage 2, these Results and their Projects need to be at least loosely linked to the desired Uses and Benefits prior to a more rigorous and *Validated* linking in Stage 3: Develop Evidence-Based Strategies.
3. These Projects and Results could be existing and/or proposed Projects and Results to create a new strategy or to audit an existing strategy.

THE START-TO-FINISH ACTION SEQUENCE FOR STAGE 2

1. Start Stage 2 by sharing with all potential suppliers and purchasers the information from Stage 1:
    a. Values and Fundamental Principles.
    b. The Uses and Benefits *as defined by the end-users*.
    c. Indications of what end users believe they need (Results) in order to enable and motivate their Uses.
2. Facilitate suppliers to identify potential Projects that will produce the *right* set of necessary and sufficient Results that will *'enable and motivate the previously identified Uses to create Benefits'*.
3. Invite suppliers to offer different Results that might enable different but equally Worthwhile Uses and Benefits.
4. Correlate the Projects and Results with the Uses and Benefits.

5.   Identify and if possible collect cause-and-effect Evidence that would compellingly support the linking of the potential Projects and Results to the desired Uses and Benefits.

6.   Identify performance indicators which can subsequently be used to monitor and *manage* the Projects to create Results and to *influence* the Uses to create Benefits.

7.   Cross-check that the desired Projects, Results, Uses and Benefits still align with the agreed Values and Fundamental Principles.

Stage 3: Develop Evidence-based strategies

WHAT IS STAGE 3?

Stage 3 consists of logically linking Projects and Results to Uses and
Benefits and adding compelling cause-and-effect Evidence that:

1.   the Projects really will create the Results;
2.   the Results really will enable and motivate the Uses;
3.   the Uses really will create the Benefits.

WHAT STAGE 3 WILL ACHIEVE IN ORDER TO SUPPORT THE OTHER EIGHT STAGES

1.   An integrated set of potential and/or existing SubStrategies,
        each one being logical and supported by compelling cause-
        and-effect Evidence.
2.   Generally, this set of SubStrategies will consist of:
        a.   a high-level Aspirational-level SubStrategy which cap-
                tures on one page (15 +/– 5 PRUB boxes) the overall
                intentions of the strategy;
        b.   a set of Guidance-level SubStrategies which provide
                more detail of what is intended without getting into the
                day-to-day operational detail (see Stage 7: "Implement
                Strategies" for information on Operational-level
                SubStrategies).
3.   In the case of auditing an existing strategy, this Stage (3) will
        test the validity of the existing set of SubStrategies and indi-
        cate if the current SubStrategies are or are not:
        a.   logical;
        b.   supported by compelling Evidence that they are actu-
                ally working.

THE START-TO-FINISH ACTION SEQUENCE FOR STAGE 3

1.   **DRIC**. Use DRIC to refine the *logic* of the rough SubStrategies
        arising from Stage 2. DRIC = **D**istil; **R**efine; **I**nfer; **C**reate
        (*Validating Strategies*, page 162).
        a.   **Distil**. Review the rough SubStrategies from Stages
                1 and 2 and distil those Projects, Results, Uses and

Benefits which meet the criteria for the purchaser and its stakeholders.

b.   **Refine**. Reword the Projects, Results, Uses and Benefits so that they are succinct and crystal clear and can be understood by all stakeholders.

c.   **Infer**. Infer missing Projects, Results, Uses and Benefits where it is straightforward to do so.

d.   **Create**. Create new Projects, Results, Uses and Benefits to fill any remaining gaps in the SubStrategy.

2.   **Validate**. Add cause-and-effect Evidence to every Link to confirm that the SubStrategies *really will work*.

3.   **Performance indicators:** Fine-tune the performance indicators associated with each Project, Result, Use and Benefit so that *progress* (lead indicators) and *success* (lag indicators) are clearly defined.

Stage 4: Validate strategies by determining their Worth

WHAT IS STAGE 4?

Stage 4 consists of:

1. Confirming that the consolidated Worth of all the Benefits is greater than the costs of all the Projects *plus* the costs of all the Uses (Global Worth).
2. Confirming that each and every stakeholder obtains sufficient Worth to motivate them to make their necessary contributions to implementing the strategy (Motivational Worth).

WHAT STAGE 4 WILL ACHIEVE IN ORDER TO SUPPORT THE OTHER 8 STAGES

Stage 4 will generate:

1. An integrated set of potential, *Validated* SubStrategies, each one compellingly demonstrating that the total consolidated *Worth* of all the Benefits is greater than the costs of all the Projects *plus* the cost of all the Uses (Global Worth).
2. The suite of *Validated* SubStrategies must *also* demonstrate that every stakeholder (especially end-users) who is required to contribute to the success of the SubStrategy will gain sufficient *Worth* to motivate their contributions. This means that the Worth of the Benefits to each key stakeholder must be greater than the costs *to them* of the Projects *plus* the costs *to them* of the Uses (Motivational Worth).

THE START-TO-FINISH ACTION SEQUENCE FOR STAGE 4

1. Identify, quantify and add up the costs of each Project.
2. Identify, quantify and add up the true costs to each user of each Use and multiply by the number of users and frequency of Uses.
3. Calculate the Global and Motivational Worth of the Benefits and hence the 'Worth' of the SubStrategy both globally and to each stakeholder.

4.   If necessary, upgrade the SubStrategy so that:
     a.   it will produce sufficient Global Worth;
     b.   it will produce sufficient Motivational Worth for each
          and every key stakeholder.
5.   If sufficiently compelling, Motivational Worth cannot be cre-
     ated then, *as a last resort,* consider if some form of regulation
     or coercion can be applied to 'encourage' those stakeholders to
     contribute as required to implementing the SubStrategy.
6.   Confirm the most relevant performance indicators and asso-
     ciated targets associated with each Project, Result, Use and
     Benefit.

Stage 5: Make investment decisions

WHAT IS STAGE 5?

Stage 5 consists of comparing multiple *Validated* SubStrategies (SubStrategies that are simultaneously logical, Evidence-based and Worth it) and selecting those that best fit the investment criteria of the various decision makers.

WHAT STAGE 5 WILL ACHIEVE IN ORDER TO SUPPORT THE OTHER 8 STAGES

1. General investments: A prioritised list of SubStrategies that stakeholders have *collectively* agreed to invest in.
2. Subgroup investments: A set of other SubStrategies that individuals or subgroups of stakeholders have agreed to invest in.

THE START-TO-FINISH ACTION SEQUENCE FOR STAGE 5

1. Stakeholder groups and subgroups establish their own standards for the *relative Worth* of economic, social, environmental and cultural Global and Motivational Worth.
2. Check that these relative Worths align with the group's agreed overall Values and Fundamental Principles.
3. Check that each business case (*Validated SubStrategy*) is fully *Validated* in the context of the newly determined *relative Worths*.
4. Prioritise investments in SubStrategies using the three-step process recommended in *Validating Strategies*, page 105–108:
    a. voting;
    b. clustering of subgroups;
    c. clustering of SubStrategies.
5. For major SubStrategies, probably undertake more comprehensive analyses using methods such as Better Business Case or Investment Logic Mapping as referenced earlier.
6. Reconfirm the most relevant performance indicators and associated targets associated with each Project, Result, Use and Benefit so that they can be used to monitor the agreed priority Worths.

Stage 6: Create performance-based contracts

WHAT IS STAGE 6?

Stage 6 consists of agreeing and documenting exactly:

1.   who will do what; when; where; why; and how;
2.   the ways that these will be performance-managed;
3.   how contributors will be rewarded;
4.   legal factors.

WHAT STAGE 6 WILL ACHIEVE IN ORDER TO SUPPORT THE OTHER 8 STAGES

Stage 6 will produce crystal clear contracts which include:

1.   All elements of the business case (the SubStrategy; the cause-and-effect Evidence; the Global and Motivational Worths).
2.   Clear identification of the PRUB-Effectiveness and PRUB-Efficiency accountabilities in terms of performance management, i.e.:
   a.   what indicators will be monitored;
   b.   identifying and distinguishing lead and lag indicators;
   c.   what their target values are;
   d.   what actions will be taken if targets are being missed;
   e.   who is responsible for each category of accountability.
3.   Traditional legal elements of contracts such as confidentiality, relevant laws, the country of jurisdiction, variations' procedures, disputes resolution procedures, contact details and so on.

THE START-TO-FINISH ACTION SEQUENCE FOR STAGE 6

Stages 1 to 5 have created well-*Validated* SubStrategies with clearly defined accountabilities and selected the best ones to support and implement. It should now be straightforward to encapsulate those SubStrategies into contract documents by drafting them in legally enforceable formats.

1.   The PRUB-related components:
   a.   Import into the contracts the *Validated* SubStrategies and accountabilities from Stage 5.

b.   If necessary, develop *sub*-SubStrategies that define more detailed contractual steps, especially in relation to Projects and their milestones.

c.   Distribute the elements of the *sub*-SubStrategies appropriately between contracts with different suppliers while ensuring that these contracts complement each other in an integrated way.

2.   The non-PRUB-related components:

a.   Encapsulate the *Validated* SubStrategies and accountabilities in the traditional legal components of a contract (country of jurisdiction; the laws governing the contract; confidentiality, ownership of intellectual property and so on).

Stage 7: Implement strategies

WHAT IS STAGE 7?

In Stage 7 stakeholders do *with confidence* the right things in the right ways that *enable and motivate Uses to create Benefits* – so that their approved suite of Validated SubStrategies will be effective and efficient.

Stage 7 typically consists of (many) stakeholders running (many) Projects to produce (many) Results that enable and motivate (many) Uses to create (many) Benefits which have both Global Worth plus Motivational Worth for each and every stakeholder who needs to contribute to the success of the strategy implementation.

WHAT STAGE 7 WILL ACHIEVE IN ORDER TO SUPPORT THE OTHER 8 STAGES

Stage 7 will:

1. *create Results that enable and motivate Uses to create Benefits;*
2. create information that can be used (in parallel or in sequence with Stage 8) to performance-manage this implementation and in Stage 9 to update the SubStrategies.

THE START-TO-FINISH ACTION SEQUENCE FOR STAGE 7

1. Develop operational-level project management *sub*-SubStrategies and plans based on the contractually defined SubStrategies with their performance management and accountability criteria from Stage 6.
2. Interlink these SubStrategies so that their implementation is complementary.
3. *Manage* Projects in well-controlled ways to efficiently create effective Results.
4. *Influence* Uses to efficiently create effective Benefits.
5. Generate information that can be used in Stage 8 to monitor and improve performance and to review the overall performance of the strategy in Stage 9.

Stage 8: Performance-manage strategies

WHAT IS STAGE 8?

Stage 8 consists of monitoring the implementation of *current* Projects, Results, Uses and Benefits to check that they are evolving as contracted. If not, then Stage 8 improves the Projects to more efficiently produce more useable Results which better *enable and motivate Uses to create Benefits*. So, Stage 8 focuses on improving *efficiency* in the *current* strategy.

In contrast to this Stage 8, Stage 9 *reviews the overall strategy itself to check if it is still the most effective strategy* and updates it to make it more appropriate and effective or even replaces it with a better strategy. Stages 8 and 9 invariably overlap but for clarity they are discussed separately here.

So, Stage 8 focuses on *efficiency in the current strategy* (doing current things right) and Stage 9 focuses on *effectiveness of the current and future strategies* (doing the right things even if that means doing new things).

WHAT STAGE 8 WILL ACHIEVE IN ORDER TO SUPPORT THE OTHER EIGHT STAGES

1. Stage 8 *must* include performance *management* and not just monitoring ('You do not fatten the pig by measuring it').

2. Stage 8 will stimulate and guide the implementation (in Stage 7) of new actions being taken by suppliers where this is necessary due to the implementation of the contracted SubStrategies turning out to be less *efficient* than expected. So, Stage 8 focuses on identifying *how the contracted SubStrategies are being implemented* and what needs changing to improve the *efficiency*, not on whether or not they are the best SubStrategies (that is done in Stage 9).

3. Stage 8 will identify where SubStrategies are turning out to be less *effective* than expected. This information will underpin robust decisions on making changes to the SubStrategies in Stage 9. To make such decisions it may be necessary to revisit Stages 1 to 7 in order to update the strategies, decisions, contracts and implementation to achieve the desired Benefits.

4. Decisions must be based on robust monitoring information of both lead and lag indicators (respectively: indicators/targets/ measurements for Projects/Results and for Uses/Benefits).

Lead indicators are measures of *progress* whereas lag indicators are measures of *success*.

5.   Project teams implement the new, efficiency-enhancing decisions back in Stage 7.

THE START-TO-FINISH ACTION SEQUENCE FOR STAGE 8

1.   Determine if the contractually specified indicators, Evidence and targets are still relevant for monitoring and managing individual SubStrategies *and* for monitoring and managing the interactions between SubStrategies, and agree on a final set of indicators and targets.

2.   Inform all stakeholders of the indicators, Evidence and targets for each Project, Result, Uses and Benefit and reconfirm with them why it is important to collect this information.

3.   Monitor the performance indicators and the cause-and-effect Evidence sufficiently often to underpin decision making to improve the performance of existing strategies in Stage 7 and to improve or create new strategies in Stage 9.

4.   Decision makers make wise, performance-enhancing decisions based on reliable performance monitoring information and on cause-and-effect Evidence.

5.   Project teams implement the new, performance-enhancing decisions.

Stage 9: Review and update strategies

WHAT IS STAGE 9?

Stage 9 consists of regularly reviewing the SubStrategies (from Stage 3) and their implementation and performance management (Stages 7 and 8) to check that they are still current and if necessary, updating them. If done rapidly and repeatedly, this correlates with 'Agile' development.

Stage 8 focused on the *performance management of the efficiency of implementing the current SubStrategies.*

This Stage 9 focuses on *whether or not the current SubStrategies were the most effective ones.*

Stage 9 also provides an audit trail of evolving SubStrategies which highlight what worked and what did not work so that lessons that have been learned are not lost.

WHAT STAGE 9 WILL ACHIEVE IN ORDER TO SUPPORT THE OTHER EIGHT STAGES

Stage 9 will produce a thorough summary of exactly where the current SubStrategies worked effectively or worked ineffectively so as to guide the development of better SubStrategies. Success/failure will be evident if actual Results, Uses and Benefits are the same as/differ from those predicted by the original SubStrategies.

THE START-TO-FINISH ACTION SEQUENCE FOR STAGE 9

This review process will start by reviewing whether or not the desired Benefits were or are being *effectively* achieved. The key questions that need to be asked are:

1. If the SubStrategies created the desired Benefits, would refined SubStrategies enable more/better Benefits for lower cost?
2. If the SubStrategies did not create the desired Benefits, then:
   a. Did the Uses happen as expected but the Benefits did not arise? If so, then *the wrong Uses were chosen in the SubStrategy,* so you need to enable better/different Uses.
   b. Did the Uses not happen as expected so the Benefits did not arise? If so, then *the wrong/insufficient Results*

were created that did not enable/motivate the Uses, so you
need to create better/different Results.

3.   If the SubStrategies did not enable the desired Uses, then:

    a.   Were the desired Results available but did not get
used? If so, then *the wrong/insufficient Results were chosen in the SubStrategy,* so you need to create better/dif-
ferent/more Results. If the right physical Results were
not Used then it may be that they were *insufficient,* e.g.,
the right physical Results might have been available
but maybe no one knew about them (so, a marketing Project-Result needs to be added) or maybe they
weren't accessible (so, maybe new transport/parking
options need to be added).

    b.   Did the intended Results not get created? If so, then *the
wrong Projects were run,* so you need to run better/dif-
ferent Projects to produce the intended Results.

Glossary

The glossary of terms from *Validating Strategies* Appendix 1 pages 197–210 is repeated below. To that glossary, I now add the following definitions in order to unequivocally distinguish between 'Values' and 'values' (which we replace with 'Worths').

Values

These are 'principles or standards of behaviour; one's judgement of what is important in life' (the second definition in: https://www.google.com/search?q=Values&oq=Values&aqs=chrome..69i57.1045j0j7&sourceid=chrome&ie=UTF-8)

'Values' are not the same as 'the value of something' which, to avoid confusion, we define as 'Worths' as follows.

Worths

Worths are a measure of how Worthwhile a Benefit is perceived to be by a stakeholder who gains that Benefit. Previously, I and many others have referred to these Worths as 'values' but this has proven to be confused with 'Values' as described above. We therefore now use the following terminology:

> **Global Worth:** The consolidated Worth of all the Benefits in each SubStrategy or business case divided by the sum of the costs of all the Projects plus the costs of all the Uses in each SubStrategy. Global Worth must be positive in order for a SubStrategy to be Validated

> **Motivational Worth:** The net Worth of a SubStrategy to each stake-
> holder. Motivational Worth must be positive for each and
> every stakeholder for a SubStrategy to be Validated

The following pages provide an updated glossary of OpenStrategies terminology as first published in *Validating Strategies – Linking Projects and
Results to Uses and Benefits*.

Active/passive

Uses can be written as active or passive Uses. OpenStrategies strongly rec-
ommends that all Uses are written as active Uses in order to confirm that
it is the actions of end-users which make a strategy successful.

Aspirational SubStrategies

These are the highest-level strategies and describe what stakeholders
aspire to. They typically describe desired outcomes without defining in
detail how these outcomes will be achieved.

High-level Aspirational SubStrategies are brief documents which
capture the general principles and desired outcomes of a strategy.
Aspirational strategies are typically valuable to politicians and business leaders who are focused primarily on 'the big picture' or 'vision'
for a strategy. Aspirational strategies can be defined as SubStrategies
but they don't contain enough detail to enable them to be Validated or
implemented.

In essence, Aspirational SubStrategies are generally broad statements
of purpose with limited specificity in terms of:

- themes (what will be done);
- demography (who it is being done for);
- geography (where it is being done);
- organisations (who will do it).

Benefits

Benefits are the desired consequences of Uses done by citizens, customers, the community or the environment. They are the final goal within

any strategy and are sometimes called 'outcomes' in other strategy documents.

Budget

The budget identifies the resources (especially financial resources) that will be required to enable a Project to proceed.

BURP

This acronym is used to denote the four types of OpenStrategies Items (PRUB-Logic) in reverse order: Benefits, Uses, Results and Projects. Items are often recorded in this order when the focus is first and foremost on defining the desired Benefits for a community or when the focus is more on developing strategy and less on recording existing activities.

Collaboration

In this book, we use the term collaboration to refer to the involvement of stakeholders during the implementation of a strategy and not just when stakeholders are merely talking together.

Compound Uses

Every Use involves multiple steps. These steps can be written as a 'simple Use' (for example, 'students learn new information during classes') or as multiple steps in a 'compound Use' (for example, 'students listen to their tutors, complete exercises and do homework in order to learn new information').

Effectiveness

In the OpenStrategies system, 'Effectiveness' is defined as 'doing the right things' as distinct from 'Efficiency' which is 'doing things right'.

Efficiency

In the OpenStrategies system, 'Efficiency' is defined as 'doing things right' as distinct from 'Effectiveness' which is 'doing the right things'.

End-point PRUB Item

'End-point' Items are 'one-off' completed Items with a fixed point of completion (or application or availability). They can be quantified or measured. For example, an 'end-point' Result could be 'a cycle-track' as this would be the end-point of a Project to 'build a cycle-track'. Hopefully, it would not be the end-point of a SubStrategy involving a cycle-track because such a SubStrategy should include the ongoing Use of the cycleway as well as the ongoing Benefits to be derived from that Use.

End-users

In the OpenStrategies system, end-users are the people, communities, organisations and the environment that Use the Results (assets) created by service providers.

Engagement

In this book we use the term engagement to refer to the involvement of stakeholders during the development of a strategy. Ideally, such stakeholders will continue to be involved throughout the implementation of the strategy.

Evidence and PRUB-Evidence

In the OpenStrategies system, the term Evidence refers to information which provides confidence that the Links in an OpenStrategy are in fact true and will happen in practice.

A SubStrategy or OpenStrategy only has real value if there is compelling cause-and-effect Evidence that the statements it contains are true or very likely to be true. This is particularly so in relation to having solid Evidence that Results will in fact be Used by customers/communities/citizens/the environment and that such Uses will generate Worthwhile Benefits. It is also crucially important to have firm Evidence that adoptable Orphan Results are in fact going to be Adopted.

Evidence 'resides' in the Links in a SubStrategy.

Cause-and-effect Evidence is not the same as performance measurement data (see section 2.10 in *Validating Strategies*). Cause-and-effect Evidence provides information on the impact a Project has on a Result or a Result has on a Use or a Use has on a Benefit. In contrast, performance measurement simply measures parameters within each Project, Result, Use and Benefit and does not contain cause-and-effect information. This information is not Evidence of cause and effect – it is simply a measure of the 'effect'.

When seeking compelling Evidence to help validate a strategy, it is essential to know 'what caused what' to happen (that is, Evidence) rather than to merely measure the 'consequences of what happened' (performance measurement data).

Understanding cause-and-effect Evidence is a key component of effective risk management.

Evolving PRUB Item

An evolving Item implies the prospect of continuing change and improvement; the focus is on changes that happen over a (sometimes specified) period of time. An example of an evolving Use could be: 'Each year a further 1% of the local population attends the health clinic'.

Fundamental Principles

Fundamental principles are core concepts which apply to all actions and consequences in a strategy. For example, they may relate to a 'commitment to public participation' in a strategy or a 'commitment to ecological sustainability'. As such they are not actions or consequences but instead they describe 'ways of behaving'.

Guidance SubStrategies

Mid-level Guidance SubStrategies are documents which flesh out an Aspirational SubStrategy in sufficient detail so that people understand broadly what needs to be done but they do not provide enough detail to enable implementation. Typically they outline what will be done and provide limited information on who it is being done for, where it is being done and who will implement the strategy.

Guidance SubStrategies are valuable to senior operational managers to enable budgeting, planning and inter-organisational collaboration.

Guidance SubStrategies provide more information on the four key 'specificities' (thematic, demographic, geographic and organisational) than do Aspirational SubStrategies but they still do not get into operational details so they cannot be directly implemented.

Issues

Issues are themes or topics which are the focus of SubStrategies or an OpenStrategy. They typically generate a number of different PRUB Items and sometimes entire SubStrategies or sequences of PRUBs.

Items

An Item is one of the four elements making up the PRUB structure and is a Project, a Result, a Use or a Benefit.

Links: positive and negative

In the PRUB structure, when one Item contributes to another a Link is formed as indicated by arrows. The Link between two Items may be positive, negative or neutral.

A positive Link indicates that the first item will increase the likelihood of the second Item occurring or increase the extent to which it occurs.

A negative Link indicates that the first item will decrease the likelihood of the second Item occurring or reduce the extent to which it occurs.

If it is not possible to establish Links between Items in a SubStrategy, this provides an indication that something is wrong with the SubStrategy and needs investigation.

Necessary and sufficient

In order to enable and motivate Uses, Results must be both necessary and sufficient. This means that:

- the Results must physically exist, and
- the physical Results may need to be supported by a skilled practitioner, and
- Users need to know about the Results, and
- Users need to comprehend the Results, and
- Users need to access the Results, and
- Users need to afford the Results, and
- Users need to know how to use the Results, and
- Users need to be motivated (by the Worth of the Benefits they gain) to use the Results

Only when the set of Results addresses all the above bullet points is the set of Results both necessary and sufficient.

Ongoing PRUB Item

Ongoing Items have no fixed 'end-point' of availability or application. Such Items are not or cannot easily be quantified or measured and may continue indefinitely. A typical ongoing Use could be: 'people continue to visit the museum'.

Operational SubStrategies

Operational SubStrategies are comprehensive and detailed action plans which specify exactly what will be done, who it is being done for, where it is being done and who will implement the strategy. They are valuable to the people who actually make things happen. Operational SubStrategies contain enough detail to enable them to be Validated and implemented.

Operational strategies provide sufficiently detailed information on each of the four specificities (thematic, demographic, geographic and organisational) so that anyone reading the operational strategy would know exactly what to do to implement it.

OpenStrategy(ies)

An OpenStrategy is a strategy that has been translated into PRUB items in the form of an interlinked suite of SubStrategies, audited for gaps, repetition, lack of clarity, and so on, and then Validated using the PRUB-Validate process (see Chapter 6 in Validating Strategies). There is no strict dividing line between a SubStrategy and an OpenStrategy other than that a SubStrategy is usually smaller and is focused on a single issue, whereas an OpenStrategy is more likely to address many interlinked themes. An OpenStrategy will ideally consist of:

- a set of Values;
- a set of Fundamental Principles which reflect those Values;
- an Aspirational SubStrategy;
- a set of Guidance-level SubStrategies;
- a set of Operational-level SubStrategies;
- and probably some narratives.

OpenStrategy diagnosis

An OpenStrategy diagnosis is the audit of strategies to assess whether they satisfy the rules of SubStrategies and OpenStrategies.

Orphan Results – see under 'Results' below
Performance measurement and management

In the OpenStrategies system, performance indicators, targets and measurements reside within each PRUB Item (see Chapter 2):

- Indicators define the performance parameters that are to be measured.
- Targets define the desired performance for each indicator.
- Measurements are the actual measurements of each indicator.

Placeholder PRUB Item

A placeholder Item is used when creating a SubStrategy and you are not yet clear about the exact wording of a Project, Result, Use or Benefit. A placeholder Item captures the fact that a Project, Result, Use or Benefit needs to be defined and in so doing it captures an idea without needing it to be fully defined.

Pooled budgets vs. joined-up budgets

OpenStrategies distinguishes between pooled budgets and joined-up budgets as follows:

> Pooled budgets are where stakeholders' budgets are consolidated into a central pool of resources which are then allocated to SubStrategies by a committee of stakeholders. Stakeholders then have no direct accountability for where their own specific resources are allocated.

> Joined-up budgets are where stakeholders selected SubStrategies or parts of SubStrategies to which they will supply their own resources in collaboration with other stakeholders who are similarly selecting and implementing SubStrategies. Stakeholders retain direct accountability for where their resources are allocated while still working collaboratively.

Projects

Projects are actions or activities undertaken to create and/or maintain assets (Results).

PRUB-Logic

The PRUB acronym denotes the four types of OpenStrategies Item: Projects, Results, Uses and Benefits. Items are often recorded in this order when, prior to developing SubStrategies, a record of existing Projects and activities is desired. This order is also useful when the focus is on implementing a strategy or SubStrategies. The entire OpenStrategies system is based on PRUB-Logic.

PRUB-Validate

PRUB-Validate (see Chapter 6 in *Validating Strategies*) is a four-step process for creating Validated SubStrategies. It can also be used to evaluate existing strategies to determine whether or not they can be Validated.

PRUB-Validate Diagnosis

A PRUB-Validate Diagnosis is a Project-by-Project diagnosis of real Projects that are ready and able to be implemented in order to assess whether they will genuinely lead via Results and Uses to Benefits and whether or not this sequence will be Worth doing.

PRUB Validation Index

The *PRUB Validation Index* is a set of three numbers which represent:

1.   how logical the SubStrategy is (on a score of 1–5);
2.   how strong the Evidence for all the Links in the SubStrategy is (on a score of 1–5);
3.   how Worthwhile the SubStrategy is (on a score of 1–5).

Results

Results are the consequences of Projects and are in place to be 'handed over' to the end-users (customers, citizens and communities) to Use to create Benefits.

There are basically two main categories of Result:

- A usable Result that is able to be used directly and immediately by end-users.
- An unusable Result that is not able to be used directly and immediately (Orphan Result).

There are some powerful subtleties relating to the types of Results (both usable and unusable), as follows:

- A usable Result is one that is ready to be handed over and used by end-users; it may or may not be sufficient, it may or may not be necessary, and it may or may not be wanted.
- An unusable Result is one where there are obstacles to its use and where some sort of modification needs to be made before it can become a usable Result.
- A necessary Result is one which must be present in order to achieve the desired Use and Benefit. A necessary Result is both usable and wanted.
- An unnecessary Result is one where something sufficiently similar already exists or where the unnecessary Result is simply not required.
- A sufficient Result has everything ready for handover to the end-users: nothing is missing and no further steps are needed before the handover can occur.
- An insufficient Result is one that is not currently being used but which could be used once it has been modified or further developed in some way or where, if accompanied by other Results, it could be part of a sufficient set of Results.
- A wanted Result is one which the community sees as having both Global and Motivational Worth and thus is something they want to Use. A wanted Result should be usable, may or may not be necessary and should be sufficient.
- An unwanted Result is one which lacks any Evidence of community or customer need or desire and where subsequently there is no pick-up or Use by the community or customers.
- An Abandoned Orphan Result is one which cannot or will not be used in any way whatsoever, either internally by the organisation or by clients or the community.

- An Adopted Orphan Result is one which cannot be directly used by end-users but which contributes to other Projects and so is used to create further Results – which may, in turn, create more Adopted Orphan Results and/or directly useable Results.
- An internal Result refers to the use of Adopted Orphan Results which are used internally to contribute to another Project (note that no capital letter is used for 'internal use'; 'Use' with a capital letter refers only to 'Use' by end-users).

Scalability

Scalability refers to the ability of a process to operate at multiple levels. The OpenStrategies system is scalable in a number of ways, including:

- being effective for multiple levels of strategies (Aspirational, Guidance and Operational).
- being effective for strategies ranging from small single-issue SubStrategies up to large multi-stakeholder, multi-themed strategies affecting many categories of people.
- enabling collaboration at the level of small single-issue SubStrategies up to large multi-stakeholder, multi-themed strategies affecting many categories of people.

Service providers/suppliers

In the OpenStrategies system, service providers/suppliers are the organisations and individuals who run Projects to produce Results (assets). Service providers/suppliers can be companies, government departments, local government agencies, voluntary agencies, individual citizens, the environment and anyone else who creates assets which are to be Used.

Strategy

A strategy is a plan and an Evidence-based rationale for that plan.

Strategy Environment Diagnosis

A Strategy Environment Diagnosis consists of identifying all strategy requirements for a stakeholder group, defining how they do or should interlink, clarifying the quality of these strategies and interlinks and recommending actions for creating an effective OpenStrategy.

A Strategy Environment Diagnosis will also identify the key characteristics of a strategy environment, for example, whether the strategic environment is predominantly simple, complicated, complex or chaotic. A Strategy Environment Diagnosis should be performed before any strategies are created.

SubStrategies

In the OpenStrategies system, a SubStrategy is a small-scale strategy usually on a single theme or for a single demographic group of end-users or for a single geographic area. An interlinked suite of multiple SubStrategies constitutes an OpenStrategy.

SubStrategies are small sets of PRUBs which typically focus on a specific topic or demographic group. If they are at an Aspirational or Guidance level, they cannot be directly implemented. If they are at an Operational level, they can be directly implemented.

SubStrategies may be created in their own right or they may be distilled from larger broad-themed OpenStrategies in order to focus attention on specific topics. SubStrategies can be created from other strategy documents by applying the PRUB translation principles of Distilling, Refining, Inferring and Creating (DRIC – see Chapter 6 in this book).

Translate: Distil + Refine + Infer + Create (DRIC)

When working with existing strategy documents or material with a view to translating the text into PRUB-Logic (and possibly forming SubStrategies), you apply the skills of distilling and refining PRUB Items, inferring meaning from those parts of the strategy document where the meaning is unclear, ambiguous or incomplete and creating new PRUB Items where necessary to create coherent SubStrategies.

- Distil – this involves taking apart and breaking down existing strategy text into PRUB-Logic without changing the wording of the original text.
- Refine – this task involves modifying existing text in order to turn it into PRUB-Logic.
- Infer – this step becomes necessary when the existing text is ambiguous, imprecise or has gaps in meaning. Inferring may also take place when existing text has been omitted to 'spell out the obvious'.
- Create – this step involves the creation of new Projects, Results, Uses and Benefits in order to complete the strategy.

Transparency

In the OpenStrategies system the term transparency refers to the ease with which stakeholders can access and understand a strategy.

Uses

Uses are actions or activities done by individuals or groups of individuals or even companies or the environment who are Using an asset (created by a service provider) to create Benefits. Generally, they will be undertaking these Uses for their own Benefit, but often other people (or, for example, the environment) will also Benefit.

The main categories of Uses (see Chapter 4 in *Validating Strategies* for more details) are:

- An ongoing Use is one which continues unchanged over a period of time.
- An evolving Use is one which is changing over time.
- An emergent Use may initially not exist and people may not be aware of it as a possibility but which becomes apparent over time.
- An end-point Use is one which is completed at a particular point in time.
- A one-off Use is one which only happens once.
- An intermittent Use is one which happens from time to time.

- An optional Use (representing most Uses) is one where the users can choose to either Use or not Use one or more Results.
- A non-optional Use (very rare) is one where users are forced to Use a Result.
- An automatic or unconscious Use is one where the users have not consciously decided to Use a particular Result or Results and they may be completely unaware that they are using a new Result.
- An opt-out Use is one where people choose to Use a different Result from the ones provided for in a SubStrategy or OpenStrategy.
- An invisible Use is one which many stakeholders might totally overlook but which is nevertheless very important to some people.
- An exclusive Use is one where the Use of a Result or Results prevents other people from using the same Result(s).
- A non-exclusive Use is one where the Use of a Result or Results does not prevent other people from using the same Result(s).
- An abstractive Use is one which irreversibly consumes resources.
- A non-abstractive Use is one which does not consume resources.

Validate and PRUB-Validate

In the OpenStrategies system the term Validate means to create a SubStrategy which:

- encapsulates a logical sequence of actions and consequences from Projects through Results and Uses to Benefits;
- confirms that this logical sequence is very likely to happen by adding compelling cause-and-effect Evidence;
- confirms that it is Worth implementing this local sequence by demonstrating that the SubStrategy has a net positive Global and Motivational Worth.

Index

Note: Page numbers in *italics* indicate figures and those in **bold** indicate tables.

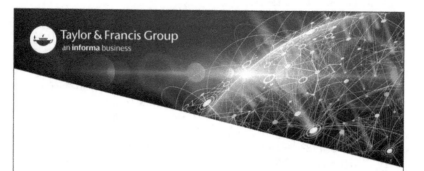